THE GULF COOPERATION COUNCIL

THE GULF COOPERATION COUNCIL

Policies, Problems and Prospects

Emile A. Nakhleh

PRAEGER

New York
Westport, Connecticut
London

To my father
my first and greatest teacher

Library of Congress Cataloging-in-Publication Data

Nakhleh, Emile A., 1938–
The Gulf Cooperation Council.

"Praeger special studies. Praeger scientific."
Bibliography: p.
Includes index.
1. Majlis al-Ta āwun li-Duwal al-Khalij al- Arabiyah.
I. Title.
DS201.M353N35 1986 341.24′77 86-8186
ISBN 0-275-92152-2 (alk. paper)

Library of Congress Catalog Card Number: 86-8186
ISBN: 0-275-92152-2

First published in 1986

Praeger Publishers, 521 Fifth Avenue, New York, NY 10175
A division of Greenwood Press, Inc.

Printed in the United States of America

The paper used in this book complies with the Permanent Paper Standard issued by the National Information Standards Organization (Z39.48-1984).

10 9 8 7 6 5 4 3 2 1

Preface

On May 25, 1981, six Arabian Peninsula states—Saudi Arabia, Kuwait, Bahrain, Qatar, Oman, and the United Arab Emirates—signed a charter creating a regional entity called "The Cooperation Council of the Arab States of the Gulf," otherwise known as the Gulf Cooperation Council (GCC). The preamble to the charter indicates that underpinning the Council are the shared religion, social and political systems, and history and aspirations of the six states. The preamble also states that although the GCC was established in May 1981, cooperation among these states and the coordination of their efforts on a regional level began many years ago, even prior to independence.

As a regional organization, the Gulf Cooperation Council is a somewhat unique experiment in the contemporary Middle East and in the Arab world in particular. It is the first regional organization in the modern Arab nation-state system, aside from the Arab League, formed in 1946, that has espoused a functional approach to cooperation while at the same time preserving the political sovereignty and independence of the member states. Since its founding, the GCC has been the focus of debate regarding its nature and functions. Intentionally or not, it has become a major media event, a fact that has contributed to the credibility gap between rising expectations based on public pronouncements and real achievements.

Officials of the six member states have repeatedly defended the organization and praised its goals. Others, including Gulf intellectuals, have questioned the wisdom of placing so many high hopes in the GCC, especially its role as a vehicle for comprehensive social, economic, and cultural development and for effective regional stability and security. Officials have argued that, through the GCC, individual states would be able to achieve collectively what they are unable to do individually and that this collective effort would be enhanced in time. Others have questioned this optimistic position on the grounds that for the GCC to succeed, it must address such knotty systemic problems as the nature of the economy, the massive numbers of expatriate workers, the small size of the indigenous population, and the absence of any popular participation in government (other than Kuwait).

This book addresses four specific aspects of the GCC: a description of its basic charter and the Unified Economic Agreement; its structure and the policy of summitry; its achievements and the challenges before it; and the official, popular, and reformist views of its proper role. On this last point, the term "reformists" includes many Gulf intellectuals, businessmen, government employees, and corporate executives who have raised serious questions about the efficacy and effectiveness of the GCC. These reformists are all indigenous citizens of the GCC states. They are highly educated, they occupy responsible positions, they are successful, and furthermore they are both beneficiaries of the present regimes and interested in the preservation of family-based rule.

The questions raised have been addressed in several studies which have been discussed at annual meetings since 1979 under the rubric of *Nadwat al-Tanmiya* or the "Development Panel for the Oil-Producing States of the Arabian Peninsula." These studies and the debates they have generated among Gulf intellectuals on developmental questions pertaining to the GCC are very exciting indeed. The *Nadwat al-Tanmiya* seems to provide the only meaningful forum for discussing the fundamental issues that will seriously affect the future success or failure of the GCC. It is a forum for educated, concerned citizens, who neither advocate the "party line" nor espouse any destructive solutions. They have basically identified the problems in GCC countries and recommended solutions. This "other" or "reformist" view of the GCC will be examined at length in this book.

In addition to the reformists, this study will examine a public opinion poll conducted in Kuwait in November 1984 concerning the GCC. This is the only poll of its kind in any GCC state that measures the people's perceptions of the GCC as a regional organization. Both the public opinion poll and the *Nadwat al-Tanmiya* studies are published only in Arabic, and have heretofore been unavailable to English-language readers.

In preparing this volume, I have relied on many sources: the published official GCC charter, agreements, and reports; statements by GCC officials; and press reports on the GCC as published in Gulf newspapers, particularly *al-Qabas* and *al-Watan* of Kuwait and *al-Khaleej* of the United Arab Emirates, and as translated in the Foreign Broadcasting Information Service (FBIS), published in Washington. I have also conducted numerous interviews with government officials in Bahrain who are directly involved as representatives of their departments in myriad GCC committees and subcommittees. In addition, I met with Gulf intellectuals–academics, businessmen, corporate executives, and government employees–who delineated some of the problems that the GCC should address. Furthermore, I have examined most of the draft studies prepared for, and discussed at, the annual meetings of *Nadwat al-Tanmiya.* Of course, all of these studies, as well as related press interviews and articles, are only available in Arabic.

A word on statistics. Most Gulf countries regard population statistics as vital information. In some countries, population figures are almost a state secret; therefore the population data can vary from one source to another. Two points should be kept in mind: First, in many cases the population figures cited in this volume are estimates; second, these figures are intended to reflect a pattern and to illustrate a point, not to represent a specific percentage.

Regarding the transliteration of Arabic names, I have attempted to spell names as they are commonly used in the Western press; I did not follow the exact transliteration system of the Library of Congress. For example, "Shaikh" is used instead of "Shaykh," "Bahrain" instead of "Bahrayn," and "Faisal" instead of "Faysal." "Amir" is used to refer to the country's ruler, such as the Amir of Kuwait. Other heads of state in the GCC context have different titles: King (Saudi Arabia); Sultan (Oman); and President (United Arab Emirates). Finally three terms are used simultaneously in this book ("Persian," "Arab," and "Gulf") to refer to the body of water separating the Arabian Peninsula and Iran. No political message whatsoever is intended in using any of these terms.

Acknowledgments

Research for this book would not have been feasible without the tremendous support I received here and overseas. I have called on many people for ideas, opinions, data, and documents. Others also helped in making the necessary preliminary arrangements for the many interviews I conducted with policymakers, intellectuals, and businessmen in the Gulf, particularly in Bahrain. My sincere thanks go to all of them.

As a professor and a department head, I could not have done all the necessary travels for this research without the support of the administration of Mount Saint Mary's College. In particular, I would like to thank the president of the college, Dr. Robert J. Wickenheiser, for awarding me two summer grants under the President's Pride faculty research program. I also want to thank Dr. John W. Campbell, Vice President for Academic Affairs, and Dr. William G. Meredith, Dean of Undergraduate Studies, for their encouragement.

In the Gulf, I would like to mention a few people whose help was essential to my research efforts on the Gulf Cooperation Council. I am particularly grateful to the following Bahraini officials: Tareq al-Moayyed, Minister of Information; Dr. Ali Fakhro, Minister of Education; Yusif al-Shirawi, Minister of Development and Industry; Dr. Husayn al-Baharna, Minister of Legal Affairs; Shaikh Muhammad bin Mubarak al-Khalifa, Minister of Foreign Affairs; and Shaikh Khalifa bin Sulman al-Khalifa, Minister of Labor and Social Affairs. I am deeply grateful for the hospitality that the Ministry of Information has extended to me on my frequent visits to Bahrain and for assisting me in scheduling interviews with government officials.

In the private sector, I will always cherish the friendship of Rod and Paula Wannebo and Jamil and Haya Wafa; their warmth and generosity have made my stay in Bahrain very pleasant. To one of my dearest friends in Bahrain and the one person who has been most encouraging of my research, Jasim Murad, I extend my heartfelt gratitude for the infinite support he has given me over the years. Jasim and his family will always be fondly remembered.

Jasim Murad's brother, Ali, and the Murads' many friends, particularly Qasim Fakhro, Hasan Fakhro, and Abdallah al-Sa'i, have all assisted me greatly in my research. I will always remember the pleasant Friday sessions at "ad-Daliya." To them go my sincere thanks.

On the home and office fronts, I am grateful to my wife for editing the manuscript, which she did cheerfully in spite of her demanding career and exhausting educational pursuits. I also want to thank my colleague and friend, Dr. Judy Ramoy Johnstone, for reading and commenting on different sections of the manuscript. Her insights and observations proved invaluable.

This manuscript could not have been done without the work of my two secretaries, Nancy Eyler and Judy Ott. I thank both of them, but I am particularly grateful for the untold hours which Nancy has spent typing and retyping the manuscript on the word processor. Her patience, dedication, and professionalism were always evident even though oftentimes the computer would have tried the patience of Job! I simply could not have met the publisher's deadline without her. I also extend my thanks to Dorothy Breitbart, Editor, Praeger Special Studies, for her useful comments throughout the writing and preparation of the manuscript.

Finally, many have contributed ideas and suggestions to this manuscript but I alone am responsible for any errors in judgment or fact that might be found herein.

Emile A. Nakhleh

Contents

List of Tables

Introduction

In reviewing the short history of the Gulf Cooperation Council, we may make several observations. First, the GCC came into being as a response to serious security-related developments in the Gulf, such as the Soviet invasion of Afghanistan, the Islamic revolution in Iran, the Iraq-Iran war, the Israeli bombing of the Iraqi nuclear reactor, and the rising threat of Islamic (Shi'ite) fundamentalist terrorism. Second, although Gulf official pronouncements have highlighted the economic, cultural, and educational goals of the GCC, and although the GCC was initially presented as another step along the already established road of cooperation among family-ruled states, it has been unable to make much impact as a regional organization apart from security.

Third, the security function of the GCC has become even more important because of the rising wave of terrorism in the region. In the Gulf context, this regional terrorism has been viewed as an attempt to replace the existing regimes with presumably pro-Iranian ones. The unsuccessful plot in Bahrain in December 1981, the bombings in Kuwait in 1984 and 1985, and the assassination attempt on the life of the Amir of Kuwait in May 1985 were all interpreted by Gulf governments as concerted moves to disrupt their countries from within. In commenting on the explosions in Kuwait in July 1985, Gulf newspapers saw a more ominous threat directed against both the GCC and the democratic experiment in Kuwait itself. (Kuwait is the only GCC state with an elected national assembly and a relatively free press.)

Fourth, since its founding five years ago, the GCC has increasingly become a media event; coverage has been promoted both by Gulf governments and by the GCC secretary-general. GCC summits have also been heavily publicized through official government publications, news releases, and intensive media reports. For example, over 250 GCC-related news articles appeared in the region's media between 1981 and 1985, as reported in the FBIS *Daily Report*. Almost 40 percent of these articles dealt with security, 25 percent reported on GCC meetings, 20 percent focused on cooperation, and 15 percent discussed the efforts of the GCC to mediate the Iraq-Iran war. The different ministerial meetings, particularly those of foreign affairs and defense, have also been covered in the press.

Since 1984, the added concern with security as a result of increasing terrorism has led to more contacts among the interior ministers of the GCC. This too has been heavily publicized in the Gulf press. Consequently, a gap has developed, at least in the people's perceptions, between the media coverage and the actual achievements of the GCC, even in the field of security. For example, in spite of the council's preoccupation with security, at least as evidenced by the press coverage, the security agreement that Saudi Arabia has promoted since 1981 has not yet been signed by the member states. Kuwait still finds the agreement objectionable. In a newspaper interview in London in mid-July 1985, the Bahraini Minister of Information stated that security cooperation among GCC was taking place with or without a written agreement. So is the case with economic cooperation. Although the GCC's Unified Economic Agreement went into effect in 1983, its impact on the life of GCC citizens has yet to be felt.

Fifth, recent literature on the GCC may be divided into two categories. The first, and by far the largest, encompasses studies (books, journal articles, magazine and newspaper reports) which by and large support the GCC and view its mission optimistically. Briefly, these studies maintain that:

1. The GCC is a natural development in the evolution of cooperation among the similar social systems of the Gulf.
2. The GCC will help the small member states achieve certain goals collectively, which could not be achieved individually.
3. In the face of outside threats and internal disruptions, these states must unite their efforts to survive.
4. On a nationalist level, the GCC is a viable vehicle for the promotion of Arab unity and the protection of the identity of the Arab population internally.
5. Because of the member states' small domestic markets and diminishing oil revenues, the GCC offers a useful forum for economic cooperation and coordination.
6. Given time and encouragement, the GCC would become a successful regional organization for functional cooperation while preserving the political independence of the member states. The above position is supported by a majority of Gulf scholars and most Gulf Arab governments and by Western governments, including the United States.

The second category of GCC literature encompasses studies that have viewed the GCC from a reformist perspective. Although these studies represent a minority of scholars (approximately 30-50), they are written by Gulf nationals (Saudis, Bahrainis, Kuwaitis, Qataris, and so on) who currently hold academic and nonacademic positions in their respective states. It is important to note the indigenous background of these scholars: they are native, Sunni, and Arab.

The main thrust of these studies involves the following points:

1. For the GCC to succeed as a regional organization, a genuine developmental process must be put in motion.
2. This process must be grounded in new and comprehensive policies in education, manpower training, and economic diversification.
3. Real security cannot be achieved except through popular participation and social justice. This will involve restructuring the educational curricula by expanding the teaching of political socialization and citizenship.
4. Gulf women, who constitute almost half the population, must be given real opportunities to take their rightful place in the labor force.
5. A thorough reexamination of the economy must be initiated to break the dependency linkages between Gulf economies and the Western industrial states, particularly the United States.

In essence, these studies have expressed a cautious support of the GCC, but they have issued several fundamental challenges to the GCC. First and foremost, the GCC should transform itself from a council of rulers to a truly regional organization. Secondly, the region cannot become secure unless individual governments allow their peoples to enjoy more individual freedom, academic freedom in the universities, and freedom of expression in the society at large. From the regimes' perspective, these studies are admittedly discomforting, but in reality, they provide the only meaningful debate of the nature and future of the GCC. Since all of these studies are still in Arabic, reviewing them in this volume should be of value to English-language readers.

This book's thesis falls into the second category of studies. It is essentially fourfold:

1. The GCC is an interesting experiment in inter-Arab regional politics, and it only has a strong possibility of success if it can overcome the serious challenges it faces.
2. The GCC has yet to transform itself from a security arrangement into a functioning regional organization.

3. The credibility gap that presently exists in Gulf people's perceptions of the effectiveness of the GCC could be eliminated if GCC leaders, especially the secretariat, consciously adopted a low-key approach to media coverages of GCC events.

4. The citizens of these states must be brought more into the GCC process so that they can feel themselves part of the effort.

To many of the Gulf's policy-oriented elites, the GCC came into being primarily as a reaction to regional threats in the late 1970s and early 1980s. They believe Western democracies, particularly the United States, have supported the establishment of the GCC because they saw in it an anti-Communist front and a potential lucrative market for Western-produced weapons and defense-related technology. Some elites have also argued that the industrialized countries have equated the existence of the present Gulf regimes with continued regional stability, which would favor Western economic and strategic interests. These regimes are strengthened by the GCC, and hence the Council has received the support of the West.

With the international oil glut, the reduction in oil production, and the diminishing oil revenues, Gulf governments must become more accountable to their peoples, particularly in terms of distributing the economic pie. The Kuwaiti National Assembly has already raised serious questions about the country's international long-term financial commitments. Indeed, the National Assembly has decided to eliminate the $300 million annual subsidy to Jordan, Syria, and the Palestine Liberation Organization. The tighter the financial situation becomes in the Gulf, the more questions will be raised. Surely, the GCC governments will take notice.

THE GULF COOPERATION COUNCIL

1
AN OVERVIEW OF THE GULF COOPERATION COUNCIL (GCC)

BACKGROUND OF THE GCC

In an official communiqué issued on May 26, 1981 in Abu Dhabi, United Arab Emirates, the heads of six Gulf Arab states declared that they had agreed to form the Gulf Cooperation Council.[1] This communiqué, which came at the end of a two-day summit held in Abu Dhabi, carried the signatures of Shaikh Zayed bin Sultan al-Nhayyan (United Arab Emirates), Shaikh Isa bin Sulman al-Khalifa (Bahrain), King Khalid bin Abd al-Aziz al-Saud (Saudi Arabia), Sultan Qabus bin Said (Oman), Shaikh Khalifa bin Hamad al-Thani (Qatar), and Shaikh Jabir al-Ahmad al-Jabir al-Sabah (Kuwait).[2]

The communiqué also indicated that the GCC charter is a culmination of many previous meetings and contacts held among the heads of state and the foreign ministers of the six Gulf states. The establishment of the GCC, according to the communiqué, rests on four major assumptions:

1. Cooperation among these states is natural and has existed for many years.
2. Gulf states would be able to protect their interests much better as a regional organization than as individuals.
3. The security of the Gulf is the responsibility of its peoples and states; any foreign intervention must be rejected.
4. Stability in the Gulf is linked to peace in the Middle East and to a just resolution of the Palestine conflict, which would guarantee the legitimate rights of the Palestinian people in the context of an independent state.[3]

The announcement on May 26 was preceded by intensive contacts and meetings. Some of these contacts date back to the late 1970s. In a series of visits to the lower Gulf in December 1978, the Amir of Kuwait strongly advocated the theme of regional cooperation. Following is a summary of those meetings.

December 6, 1978. A communiqué following a meeting between the Amir of Kuwait and the King of Saudi Arabia emphasized the two rulers' "belief in working for cooperation among the two states in all fields and in keeping the region secure and stable and away from international struggle."[4]

December 9, 1978. A communiqué following the meeting between the Amir of Kuwait and the Amir of Bahrain called for "continued efforts for more cooperation and coordination among the states of the region through a unified and comprehensive political, economic, social, and educational plan."[5]

December 12, 1978. A communiqué following the meeting between the Amir of Kuwait and the Amir of Qatar stated that "the sensitive situation present in the Gulf makes it imperative for the Arab states of the Gulf to intensify their efforts for a unity agreement among themselves."[6]

December 16, 1978. A communiqué following the meeting between the Amir of Kuwait and the Amir of Abu Dhabi stated that "the common national and religious ties and the common aspirations of the Arab peoples of the region dictate that the states of the region should unify themselves."[7]

December 20, 1978. A communiqué following a meeting between the Amir of Kuwait and the Sultan of Oman stated that "in light of the new circumstances in the region, it is imperative that the Gulf Arab states arrive at the strongest cooperative agreement possible among themselves—cooperation dictated by their common Islamic faith, historical relations and their peoples' aspirations for the realization of more progress and prosperity."[8]

Indeed, following the meeting of the Gulf foreign ministers in Kuwait on February 5, 1981, the Saudi foreign minister pointed to his Kuwaiti counterpart before the press and said, "Here is the father of the [GCC] project."[9]

Several meetings were held in 1981 in preparation for the creation of the GCC. The first meeting was held February 4, 1981 in Kuwait and was attended by the foreign ministers of the six states, which later formed the GCC. At the conclusion of the meeting, they issued a communiqué declaring that in light of their similar systems, Islamic belief, and social, economic, and demographic structures, they had agreed to establish a cooperation council.[10] The foreign ministers also stated in the same communiqué that they would meet a month later to follow up on the specific structure and goals of the cooperation council.

Following this meeting, a committee of experts from the six states met twice: in Riyadh, Saudi Arabia on February 24, 1981 and in Muscat, Oman in March 4, 1981. The purpose of those meetings was to develop a draft charter and by-laws which would be reviewed and agreed upon by the foreign ministers.[11] At the conclusion of the Muscat meeting on March 18, 1981, the committee of experts had agreed on a draft charter that included three structures: a supreme council, a ministerial council, and a secretariat-general.[12]

On Monday, March 9, 1981, the foreign ministers met in Muscat (Oman) and approved the basic structure and the draft charter, with only minor changes, which had been prepared by the committee of experts. Specifically, the foreign ministers approved three documents: the by-laws of the Cooperation Council, the by-laws of the Supreme Council, and the by-laws of the Ministerial Council. The ministers also made four recommendations: (1) to hold a meeting of the Supreme Council in May and in November of every year; (2) to hold the first session of the Supreme Council in Abu Dhabi (United Arab Emirates) on May 26-7, 1981; (3) to hold a meeting of the committee of experts in Abu Dhabi on May 20, 1981 to finalize the by-laws of the Commission for Settlement of Disputes; (4) to agree in principle that the Secretary-General of the Cooperation Council should be from Kuwait.[13]

The committee of experts met in Abu Dhabi on May 19-20, 1981 to prepare for the GCC summit and to discuss the by-laws of the Commission for Settlement of Disputes. This two-day meeting was followed by a meeting of the foreign ministers in Abu Dhabi on May 23, 1981. At that meeting, the foreign ministers approved the by-laws of the Commission for Settlement of Disputes, nominated Abdallah Bishara as Secretary-General of the GCC, and prepared the agenda for the impending GCC summit.[14]

The first GCC summit was held on May 25-26, 1981 in Abu Dhabi. The meeting was indeed a historic occasion for the family-ruled states of the Gulf. It was the first time they had assembled as independent states to discuss issues that were of particular concern to them as Gulf states. Secondly, the assembly reflected both a desire that these concerns could and should be addressed in a cooperative framework and a determination that the stability of the region would be their primary responsibility.

Each delegation of the six member states included the head of state, a special adviser to the head of state, the foreign minister, the finance minister, and a scattering of high-level bureaucrats. On the second day of the summit, a "working paper on joint Gulf action" was presented. Highlights of the working paper included the following points:

1. The establishment of the GCC, coming at a most propitious time, is a response to the current historical, social, cultural, economic, political, and strategic environment.

2. The GCC is a natural culmination of a long history of cooperation.

3. The many serious challenges—economic and political—presently facing the Gulf have made joint action imperative. Regional cooperation has become vital in the present era for the preservation of stability, security, and progress.

4. Serious collective action in the Gulf will put an end to the groundless talk of a "power vacuum" in the region.

5. Arab unity has been the dream of all Arabs since World War II, and insofar as joint Gulf action brings Gulf states together, it provides a solid step toward the realization of this dream.

6. The biggest challenge facing the oil-producing Gulf states today is the need to utilize oil-generated wealth for development. Joint action within the GCC would help Gulf societies meet this challenge.[15]

Based on these points, the summit agreed to set up five ad hoc committees, headed by appropriate ministers, for social and economic planning; economic and financial cooperation; industrial cooperation; oil; and social and cultural services.[16]

The summit concluded on May 26, 1981 with a summit communiqué announcing the establishment of the Gulf Cooperation Council.

Hundreds of GCC meetings have been held throughout the six states since that founding in 1981. These meetings have involved foreign ministers, interior ministers, chiefs of staff, directors of immigration, health ministers, directors of customs, finance ministers, oil ministers, directors of scientific research institutes, education ministers, and transportation ministers. Meetings have also been held by deputy ministers, who are charged by their respective governments with the responsibility of pursuing cooperation in the GCC in their respective areas. The five committees that were originally established have also held innumerable meetings and have generated an impressive volume of recommendations.

As a result of this activity, practically every facet of government operations in the member states has been touched by the GCC. Consequently, the secretariat has expanded significantly in staffing, in activities, and in expertise. Numerous studies have been commissioned or completed, ranging from power consumption to the introduction of a new mathematics curriculum. The following list of meetings in a recent three-month period graphically illustrates the exponential increase in GCC activities.

Table 1.1 Gulf Cooperation Council: Schedule of Meetings (December 1984-February 1985)

Date	Location	Type of Meeting
December 8-9, 1984	Secretariat-Riyadh	Subcommittee on Civil Aviation
December 9-10, 1984	Qatar	Fourth meeting of the Committee on Scientific and Technological Cooperation
December 10-13, 1984	Kuwait	Panel on developing human resources in the oil sector
December 15, 1984	Secretariat-Riyadh	Sixth meeting of directors of customs
December 18-19, 1984	Kuwait	Third meeting of directors of traffic
December 23-24, 1984	Secretariat-Riyadh	Second meeting of the Committee on Medicines and Veterinary Inoculations
December 25-26, 1984	Secretariat-Riyadh	Experts in ministries of industry to discuss industrial strategy
December 29-30, 1984	Secretariat-Riyadh	Second meeting of the Committee on Study of Seeds and Preventive Treatments
January 6, 1985	Secretariat-Riyadh	Technical Committee on the Olympics
January 7, 1985	Secretariat-Riyadh	Second meeting of the heads of Olympic committees
January 6-7, 1985	Secretariat-Riyadh	Committee in Food Strategic Reserve
January 13-14, 1985	Secretariat-Riyadh	Committee on Maritime Assistance

Table 1.1 *continues*

Table 1.1 *continued*

Date	Location	Type of Meeting
January 13-14, 1985	Secretariat-Riyadh	Fourth meeting of deputy ministers on youth and sports
January 15, 1985	Secretariat-Riyadh	Third meeting of the ministers of youth and sports
January 14-16, 1985	Secretariat-Riyadh	Third meeting of computer directors
January 22-23, 1985	Secretariat-Riyadh	Joint meeting of the representatives of development funds in GCC countries and those in charge of marketing
February 3-6, 1985	Bahrain	Subcommittee on Airline Companies
February 10-11, 1985	Secretariat-Riyadh	Administrative Training and Development Directors
February 26-27, 1985	Secretariat-Riyadh	Meteorological Committee

Source: GCC Secretariat-General, Riyadh, Saudi Arabia, *Publication No. 15* [Arabic] (December 8, 1984).

According to official statements, the Gulf Cooperation Council came into being to formalize a process of cooperation already in existence among the lower states of the Gulf. The primary focus in the agreement was on economic cooperation; security was not, at least publicly, a concern uppermost in the minds of the framers. Four themes were apparent in the original communiqué.

First, the GCC was not an outgrowth of superficial slogans or tactical plans, nor was it a response to temporary circumstances. Rather, it was a response to the Gulf peoples' desire to cooperate more closely in all fields.

Second, the GCC was not designed to have an offensive posture toward other states in the region; it was, however, designed to promote Arab unity.

Third, the GCC will primarily benefit the countries of the region —peoples and leaders; it is a viable framework for regional development.

Fourth, the formalization of cooperation within the GCC framework will strengthen the member states' resolve to resist attempts by outside powers to control the revenues and resources of the region. The GCC is designed to act as a shield to protect the security and stability of the region and, by extension, the security of the larger Arab world.[17]

The remainder of this chapter will focus on the agreement itself and on the background of the member states. Regional cooperation in security and economics will be addressed in the following chapter.

CHARTER OF THE GCC: STRUCTURE AND OBJECTIVES

At their first summit in Abu Dhabi in May 1981, the heads of the six Gulf states approved four major documents: the Charter of the Gulf Cooperation Council; the By-Laws of the Supreme Council; the By-Laws of the Ministerial Council; and the By-Laws of the Commission for Settlement of Disputes. Less than a month later, the six governments approved the Joint Economic Agreement. In this section of the chapter, the GCC Charter will be analyzed. A brief mention will also be made of the relevant by-laws. The Joint Economic Agreement and the whole issue of economic cooperation will be addressed in the next chapter.

The Charter of the GCC consists of a preamble and 22 articles (see Appendix A). In the preamble, the signatories sought to highlight the common characteristics of the member states; this commonality was felt to constitute the cornerstone of the GCC.[18] According to the preamble, the GCC Charter is based on the following factors: the existence of common bonds, special relations, similar regimes, and the Islamic religion among the member states; the belief that the peoples of the Gulf have a common destiny and a unity of purpose; and the conviction that cooperation and coordination among the member states would serve the long-term interests of the Arab nation.[19] It is also in accordance with the Charter of the Arab League.[20]

The 22 articles are divided into 6 topics: (1) basic information (Articles 1, 2, 3, 5); (2) objectives (Article 4); (3) structure (Article 5); (4) functions of the main bodies within the GCC (Articles 7-16 and 18); (5) privileges and immunities (Article 17); and (6) charter implementation, amendment, and deposition (Articles 19-22).

Articles 1, 2, 3, and 5 state that the name of the new regional organization is the Gulf Cooperation Council, that its headquarters shall be in Riyadh, that it shall hold meetings in any member state, and that it shall consist of six states: Saudi Arabia, Kuwait, Bahrain, Qatar, the United Arab Emirates, and Oman. On this last point, two observations may be made. Membership in the GCC seems to be closed to all other states in the region, and only a certain type of state seems to be eligible for membership (for example, tribal, family-ruled, Sunni-ruled, and oil-producing).

The basic objectives of the GCC are defined in Article 4 of the Charter. They are

1. To achieve cooperation among the member states in all fields as a prelude to unity.

2. To strengthen the links of cooperation among the peoples of the member states in different fields.

3. To establish similar systems among the member states in all fields, including economics and finance; commerce, customs, and communications; education and culture; social welfare and health; information and tourism; and legislation and administration.

4. To stimulate scientific and technological progress in the fields of industry, mineralogy, agriculture, and marine and animal resources. Also, to establish common projects, and to encourage the cooperation of the private sector for the common good of the peoples of the member states.

An examination of Article 4 leads to several observations. First, it is interesting to note that cooperation in the area of security was not even mentioned as being among the basic objectives of the GCC. None of the six specific areas of cooperation under paragraph 3 of Article 4 touches on security. Yet security has been the most visible preoccupation of GCC leaders.

Second, Article 4 provides a foundation for further GCC cooperation in all fields. Indeed, the five technical committees were set up specifically in accordance with Article 4 of the Charter.[21] In order to achieve the objectives stated in Article 4, the heads of state decided at their first meeting to establish the following five technical committees:

1. Social and Economic Planning Committee. The basic function of this committee is to develop areas of common action in social and economic planning, to coordinate the national development plans of the member states, and to devise future plans for social and economic coordination among the six states.

2. Economic and Financial Cooperation Committee. This committee is charged with four major responsibilities: currency and financial cooperation, the movement of capital and people and the practice of economic activity among the member states, commercial exchange, and transportation and communication.[22] The committee was given the following specific responsibilities:

a. To unify investment rules and regulations in an attempt to develop a cohesive investment policy.

b. To coordinate currency and banking policies and to increase the coordination among currency and banking institutions, eventually creating a common Gulf currency.

c. To coordinate foreign financial and currency policies, particularly as they pertain to regional and international economic and development aid.

d. To establish new regulations that would guarantee citizens of all GCC states equal treatment in terms of freedom of movement, work and residency, freedom of property ownership and inheritance, and freedom of economic activity.

e. To attempt to remove hindrances blocking the free movement of resources, capital, and other means of production and to coordinate and unify customs duties and financial and commercial regulations so that citizens of any member state would be afforded the same treatment in any of the six states.

f. To remove tariff barriers among the member states regarding national products and to attempt to create a unified customs levy among these states and between them and the outside world.

g. To coordinate the export, import, and food-reserves policies of the member states.

h. To create a collective negotiating power in the field of exports and imports.

i. To cooperate in the field of sea, land, and air transportation and communication and to coordinate the building of the necessary infrastructure (for example, ports, airports, roads, power and water stations).

3. Industrial Cooperation Committee. The responsibilities of this committee include the following:

a. To coordinate all industrial activity by proposing policies that would industrialize these states on a basis of complementarity and mutual benefit.

b. To study the standardization of industrial legislation and systems among the member states.

c. To encourage local institutions to increase their industrial output to fill the needs of the member states.

d. To prepare procedures governing the importation of technology appropriate to the development needs of the member states.

e. To distribute industrial production among the member states by establishing complimentary industrial projects.

f. To establish unified programs for vocational and industrial training.[23]

4. Oil Committee. Composed of GCC ministers for foreign affairs, oil and finance, this committee is charged with two major responsibilities:

a. To coordinate all aspects of policy planning for oil and petrochemicals, including oil production, refining, marketing, pricing, and shipping, the production of natural gas, and the development of energy resources.

b. To establish a unified oil policy toward the outside world and international organizations.[24]

5. Social and Cultural Services Committee. The major responsibility of this committee is to define the common areas of activity in education, culture, health, labor, and social welfare and to establish common policies in these areas.

The GCC Charter establishes three permanent bodies and one ad hoc commission (Article 6). They are the Supreme Council, the Ministerial Council, and the Secretariat. The Commission for Settlement of Disputes, which can be instituted when necessary, is attached to the Supreme Council (Article 10, Section 1). The Commission is a recommending body only and operates at the pleasure of the Supreme Council (Article 10, Section 4).

Voting in both the Supreme Council and the Ministerial Council is based on unanimity on substantive issues and on a majority for procedural matters (Articles 9 and 13). The unanimity requirement is potentially crippling, since major resolutions can be vetoed by any member. It would therefore be very difficult for any substantive agreement to emerge in any area, from regional security to tariffs, if any state were in opposition. The Supreme Council meets regularly once a year; special sessions may be called if requested by any one member and seconded by another (Article 7).

The Supreme Council is the highest body in the GCC. It consists of the heads of the six member states. As the major policymaking structure in the organization, the Supreme Council is given ten specific responsibilities (Article 8):

1. To review matters of interest to the member states.
2. To establish major policy goals and broad policy outlines.
3. To review the recommendations, reports, studies, and projects that are submitted by the Ministerial Council for approval.
4. To review the reports and studies that the secretary-general is charged with preparing.
5. To approve the bases for dealing with other states and with international organizations.
6. To approve the By-Laws of the Commission for Settlement of Disputes and to appoint its members.

7. To appoint the secretary-general.
8. To amend the Charter of the GCC.
9. To approve the by-laws of the Supreme Council.
10. To approve the budget of the Secretariat-General.

Articles 11 and 12 of the Charter discuss the formation and functions of the Ministerial Council. It consists of the foreign ministers of the six member states. The Council meets every three months, and its presidency rotates in alphabetical order of the member states (Article 11). The Ministerial Council is charged with performing eleven major functions (Article 12):

1. To propose policies and prepare recommendations to further cooperation among the member states.

2. To encourage cooperation among the member states in all fields and to recommend related policies to the Supreme Council for approval.

3. To submit recommendations to the appropriate ministers for implementation.

4. To encourage cooperation among all segments within the member states, particularly the private sector, to expand cooperation among the member states' chambers of commerce and industry, and to facilitate the movement of indigenous workers among the member states.

5. To refer any issue pertaining to cooperation to one or more technical and/or specialized committees for further study.

6. To review any proposals related to amending the Charter and to refer such proposals to the Supreme Council for action.

7. To approve its own by-laws as well as the by-laws of the Secretariat.

8. To appoint, upon the recommendation of the secretary-general, the Assistant Secretaries-General for a renewable three-year term.

9. To approve periodic reports and regulations relating to financial, monetary, and administrative affairs proposed by the secretary-general and to submit the budget of the Secretariat to the Supreme Council for action.

10. To arrange for the Supreme Council's meetings and to prepare their agendas.

11. To review matters referred by the Supreme Council.

The Secretariat is headed by a secretary-general and sufficient staff to carry out the functions of the Council. The staff, which is appointed by the secretary-general, must be citizens of the member states (Article 14).

As the chief administrator of the GCC, the secretary-general performs several functions, including the preparation of studies, reports, recommendations, budgets, administrative procedures, and any other tasks entrusted to him either by the Supreme Council or the Ministerial Council (Article 15). To date, the GCC has had only one secretary-general, a citizen of Kuwait, who is presently serving a second three-year term. As members of the Secretariat, the secretary-general and his staff function as regional bureaucrats with the primary responsibility of furthering the interests of the Gulf Cooperation Council. They are not representatives of their individual countries. In the performance of their duties, they are not to be subjected to influence or pressure from any member state. They are also pledged not to reveal any secrets that might damage the GCC, either during or after their tenure in office (Article 16).

The GCC, its bodies, official representatives, and employees, including the secretary-general and members of the Secretariat, are given the diplomatic privileges and immunities accorded to similar organizations under international law. The GCC has already drafted appropriate agreements between itself and the country where its headquarters are located (Article 17).

In addition to the Charter, the heads of the six Gulf states have approved by-laws for the Supreme Council, the Ministerial Council, and the Commission for Settlement of Disputes.[25] The by-laws of the Supreme Council, consisting of 19 articles, focus on the nature of the Council, the conduct of the meetings, the agenda of meetings, and voting. The by-laws further define the responsibilities assigned to the Supreme Council under the Charter.[26]

The by-laws of the Ministerial Council consist of 39 articles. Again, they focus on the internal procedures of meetings (agendas, voting, debate, and resolutions), the appointment of technical committees, and cooperation with the secretary-general. The Ministerial Council lays the groundwork for the Supreme Council.[27]

The by-laws of the Commission for Settlement of Disputes consist of 13 articles and focus on the structure, responsibilities, meetings, and deliberations of the Commission. For example, the Commission is to be headquartered in Riyadh, Saudi Arabia. The jurisdiction of the Commission falls into two areas: disputes among member states and disputes pertaining to interpreting or implementing any articles of the GCC Charter (Article 3). Being ad hoc in nature, the Commission ceases to exist whenever it submits its recommendations on a specific dispute to the Supreme Council (Article 4).[28]

STATES OF THE GCC: THE SETTING

Any analysis of the Gulf Cooperation Council must take into consideration the member states themselves. Of course, the future success or failure of the GCC will to a large extent depend on the capability, stability, self-sufficiency, and educational achievement of the member countries. Therefore it is important to note that although the six countries share many similar attributes, they also exhibit many differences.

First and foremost, it is important to remember that these states are fairly small. Their total area is under one million square miles, ranging from Bahrain, with an area of 260 square miles (the smallest), to Saudi Arabia, with an area of approximately 865,000 square miles. They stretch along the western coast of the Gulf from Kuwait in the north to Oman in the south. Of course, Saudi Arabia, extends across the entire Arabian Peninsula and borders on both the Gulf and the Red Sea.

The six states are primarily desert and experience minimal rainfall and an arid climate. Water is a precious commodity. Other than a few crops for short seasons, the GCC states are not presently self-sufficient in agriculture. Food security is a real issue and a major challenge to be overcome to secure their future independence.

Agriculture is confined to certain areas, particularly in Saudi Arabia. However, government-subsidized farming does exist in several of these countries. Today member states must import most of their foodstuffs, dairy products, and meats. Among their principal agricultural products are dates, tomatoes, melons, wheat (Saudi Arabia), onions, and sorghum. Livestock production includes sheep, goats, cattle, poultry, and camels.

In terms of population, the GCC states face major problems, including the small size of the population, a large foreign workforce, a shortage of trained indigenous workers, a lack of coherent vocational training programs, and religious divisions among the population. Although the question of population and development is discussed in Chapter 4 below, suffice it to say here that a significantly high percentage of the present populations in these states consists of foreign nationals (except Oman). When only the working population is considered, the percentage of foreign workers is even higher. Table 1.2 gives a breakdown of the population, both indigenous and foreign. The presence of massive numbers of foreign nationals is directly linked to the whole process of economic development, to long-term manpower planning, and of course to national security.

Table 1.2 Population in GCC Countries (1983 estimates)

Country	Total Population	Foreign Percent of Total	Foreign Labor Percent of Total	Literacy Percent
Bahrain	400,000	34	58	50
Kuwait	1,550,000	61	70	71
Oman	900,000	4	50	20
Qatar	267,000	80	90	50
Saudi Arabia	9,684,000	22	50	50
United Arab Emirates	1,194,000	81	90	50
Total	13,995,000			

Sources: Based on data in *The Middle East and North Africa, 1984-85* (London: Europa Publications, Ltd., 1984) and from *Background Notes* (Washington, DC: U.S. Department of State).

Economically, the GCC countries experienced an enviable boom in the 1970s and early 1980s because of a rise in the price of oil and the high international demand for oil. For over a decade, economic prosperity touched every facet of life in those countries. The abundance of petrodollars led the GCC countries to embark on massive construction programs for everything from schools to highways. A whole infrastructure for social services, public services, and industrial development was created in very few years. Demand for consumer goods increased over a thousandfold within a decade. Virtually every imaginable product has to be imported, running from toothpicks to videos. Store shelves were stacked with goods from all over the world. By 1980, the per capita GNP in the six GCC states had risen to unprecedented heights: approximately $10,000 in Bahrain, $17,000 in Kuwait, $35,000 in Qatar, $12,000 in Saudi Arabia, and $23,000 in the United Arab Emirates. Oman fell slightly behind with a per capita GNP of approximately $7,000.[29]

People, companies, construction firms, and experts descended on the Gulf from every corner of the globe. With their staggering oil revenues assured by an apparently insatiable world demand for oil and with the help of international experts in every imaginable field, the GCC countries proceeded to build modern, industrialized economies. The availability of oil and natural gas as cheap sources of energy played a pivotal role in those countries' decisions to encourage such industries as petrochemicals, fertilizers, cement, steel, and aluminum.

However, by the early to mid 1980s, a worldwide economic stagnation hit the Gulf states, and work on many projects was delayed or halted. Serious doubts began to be expressed among Gulf businessmen and others regarding the general soundness of the economic policies of some of the states. The crash of the Kuwaiti stock market (*Suq al-Manakh*) was a shock to all the Gulf states and involved close to $100 billion. Although the causes of the crash have not yet been fully revealed, it is commonly believed that many stockholders were involved in fraudulent dealings.

GCC countries were affected differently by this economic recession. The United Arab Emirates probably suffered the most, while Bahrain, because of its modest oil revenues and economic diversification, particularly in services, did not feel the full brunt of the recession. However, a quick glance at the Gulf today shows that many banks, including the offshore ones in Bahrain and elsewhere, face an uncertain future. The occupancy rate in hotels and apartment buildings is at an all-time low. Some countries, such as Saudi Arabia and Kuwait, have begun to post high deficits in their operating budgets. These deficits must then be covered from reserves. Indeed, in 1985 Saudi Arabia posted the second-largest deficit in the world, right behind the United States.

Obviously the GCC countries face a major economic challenge in their pursuit of regional cooperation, namely the type of economic planning that should be pursued in the post-oil period. Oil will not last forever; it is expected to run out within a generation in Bahrain, Qatar, and Oman, within two generations in the United Arab Emirates, and within three to four generations in Saudi Arabia and Kuwait. For the moment, however, the GCC states continue to be among the world's largest producers of oil; they also contain beneath their soil the world's largest reserves of oil and natural gas.[30] Tables 1.3 and 1.4 give a breakdown of the worldwide cumulative oil productions, and the estimated proven oil and gas reserves in the GCC states.

Most of the GCC states seem to have decided on industrialization as the focus of their post-oil economic planning. According to Professor A. A. Kubursi, a leading economist and expert on the Gulf states, industrialization serves several major purposes in the development process: diversification and self-reliance; manpower training; income generation; and technology transfer.[31]

Present industrial projects in the GCC states may be divided into three categories: oil and gas-based industries (such as petrochemicals); metal processing industries (such as aluminum and copper refining

Table 1.3 GCC Cumulative Oil Production and Proved Oil and Gas Reserves (as of January 1, 1984)

Country	Cumulative Oil Production (billions of barrels)	Estimated Oil Reserves (billions of barrels)	Estimated Gas Reserves (trillions of cubic feet)
Bahrain	0.7	0.2	7
Kuwait[1]	23.0	66.8	35
Oman	1.9	2.8	3
Qatar	3.6	3.3	62
Saudi Arabia	50.1	168.9	125
United Arab Emirates	8.6	32.3	31
Total GCC Area	87.9[2]	274.3[3]	263[4]
United States	136.3	27.3	198
Total World	515.0	669.3	3,200

[1] Includes one half of the Neutral Zone.

[2] When Iran and Iraq are added, the Gulf area's cumulative oil production equals that of the United States and accounts for 26.5 percent of total world production.

[3] With the addition of Iran and Iraq, the estimated proved reserves in the Gulf are over thirteen times those of the United States; they also account for over half of the total world oil reserves.

[4] With the addition of Iran and Iraq, the estimated proven gas reserves in the Gulf are approximately four times those of the United States and almost one fourth of the total world gas reserves.

Source: *Middle East Oil and Gas* (New York: Exxon Corporation, 1984), pp. 3-4. ©1984 Exxon Corporation; and ©1984 Westermann Druck.

and smelting); and non-oil-related consumer industries (such as foods, bakeries, confectionaries, and printing presses).[32]

Refining of crude oil is the most significant oil-based industry in the GCC countries. It gives these countries several tangible advantages: It allows them some control over the oil business downstream; it provides them with oil products for energy and industrial uses such as lubricants, asphalt, gas, oil, and naphtha; and it satisfies domestic demands for refined products. Currently, the GCC countries have a total of thirteen refineries, with a combined capacity of 1.5 million barrels per day, or 1.9 percent of the world capacity.[33] It is expected that by 1986 the GCC states would be able to refine almost 25 percent of total Gulf crude oil production.[34]

Table 1.4 GCC Crude Oil Production (thousands of barrels per day)

Country	1950	1965	1975	1980	1983
Bahrain	30	57	57	48	41
Kuwait*	344	2,351	2,087	1,661	1,076
Oman	–	–	341	282	376
Qatar	34	231	437	471	295
Saudi Arabia*	547	2,206	7,075	9,903	5,062
United Arab Emirates	–	282	1,694	1,702	1,119
Total GCC Area	955	5,127	11,691	14,067	7,969
United States	5,407	7,804	8,362	8,597	8,680
World	10,428	30,308	53,418	59,464	52,621

*Includes one half of the Neutral Zone.

Source: *Middle East Oil and Gas* (New York: Exxon Corporation, 1984), p. 5. ©1984 Exxon Corporation, and ©1984 Westermann Druck.

Another oil-based industry is natural gas liquefaction. Since 1973, most GCC states have begun to utilize their flared gases. Presently, they have concentrated on the liquefaction of propane, butane, and natural gases. By 1985, the total production capacity of the GCC region was estimated at 42,500 tons per year, of which Saudi Arabia had the lion's share.[35]

The GCC states have also expanded their petrochemical industries significantly in the last decade. The industrial chain from basic petrochemical products to final ones is complex and costly. However, given their abundance of hydrocarbons (oil and gas) and financial resources, the GCC countries are in an enviable position as regards the production of petrochemicals. They have become major producers of ethylene and propylene (used in plastics), aromatics (used in synthetic fibers), butadiene and benzene (used in rubbers), and methanol and formaldehyde (used in adhesives).[36]

In other areas of industrial production, in particular non-oil-based industries, the GCC region has made significant gains in iron and steel, aluminum, copper, and cement production. These are all energy-intensive industries, and natural gas, which could be used in these industrial processes, is available in abundance. However, the output in these industries has yet to fill the region's needs.[37]

Other industries, such as food and agricultural processing, do not hold much promise for the region, and small domestic markets are a major constraint in this area. Yet, through cooperation and careful planning on the GCC level, this type of industry might become desirable in the region.[38]

As for the political setting, the GCC states share a similar political culture and have developed similar political systems since independence. The political culture is predicated upon tribalism and Islam. The political system is based on a tribal/familial structure which is headed by an amir, chosen by the leading family within the tribe, whose rule is maintained by the continued consensus of the inner council of the family. A somewhat modern public administration and a pro-family government bureaucracy have developed in the oil era. The primary function of these agencies is to support the authority of the ruling family.

Of the six states, only Kuwait has an elected, functioning national assembly. Bahrain's one elected national assembly was dissolved in August 1975 and has not been reconvened. Qatar has a consultative assembly (*majlis shura*) whose members are appointed by the Amir. Saudi Arabia, the United Arab Emirates, and Oman have never had national assemblies.

Kuwait and Bahrain are the only two states with a permanent constitution. Qatar and the United Arab Emirates operate under provisional constitutions, whereas Saudi Arabia and Oman have no constitutions of any kind. As a traditionally religious state, Saudi Arabia has maintained that its political system is embedded in the Koran, which precludes the necessity of a written constitution. Accordingly, the Saudi king assumes three roles simultaneously: chief of state and head of the royal family; prince of the faithful (*amir al-mu'minin*); and head of all tribal shaikhs (*shaikh al-mashayikh*).

Regardless of the presence or absence of a written constitution or of a national assembly, political ideology in the GCC states has several features.[39]

First, the family rule based on the principle of hereditary succession is above popular debate.

Second, the political system is solidly based on Islam with a mainstream Sunni interpretation and a Sunni government, and on a sense of identity as Arabs. Although several wealthy Shi-ite families are members of the merchant class, they are normally not members of the higher echelons of government. Their political status is therefore not commensurate with their economic wealth.

GCC governments express their Arab identity in moderate tones and oftentimes as a matter of rhetorical habit. While they participate, often actively, in Arab League conferences and adhere to Arab League policies, they have decried the dissension and the absence of consensus among the Arab states. They have generally supported Arab causes, including the demands of the Palestinian people. However, and more importantly, the emphasis on Arab identity has been used as a shield against the influx of expatriate, essentially non-Arab, laborers. "Arab" seems to be synonymous with the "indigenous" in these countries.

Third, decision making in the political system is influenced only minimally by popular input; such input is usually transmitted informally and not as a matter of policy. No political parties, movements, or organizations are allowed to function within the body politic. In Kuwait, where parliamentary elections exist, candidates run on personal platforms rather than as members of any political parties.

Fourth, the absence of popular participation, the flow of authority from the top down, and the concentration of political power in the hands of the ruling family, all direct the political process toward the perpetuation of the status quo. Stability becomes synonymous with continued family rule, and any demands to alter the situation, no matter how genuine and how indigenous, are frowned upon, and, at worst, treated as anti-state. Government insistence on conformity with the status quo could result in curbing the rights of citizens, particularly in the face of increasing terrorism and continuing anti-Iran sentiment.

In concluding this panoramic view of the political setting, one must note that there has been no change in any of the ruling families since independence. The al-Saud family has ruled Saudi Arabia since independence in 1932. The monarchy has been held by Abd al-Aziz al-Saud, the first king, and by his children since then. The assassination of one king in 1975 and the death of another in 1982 have not threatened the continuity of the al-Saud rule.

The same pattern holds true in Kuwait, with al-Sabah family, and Bahrain, with al-Khalifa family. Qatar has also experienced a similar situation albeit with a minor change in the person of the ruler in 1972. In the United Arab Emirates, Shaikh Zayed al-Nhayyan has continued to rule as the Amir of Abu Dhabi and as president of the federation of the seven emirates. Oman has remained under the rule of Sultan Qabus since he deposed his father in the early 1970s.

In the area of defense, the GCC states, particularly Saudi Arabia, have improved their defense capability tremendously in recent years. They seem to be able to defend themselves against internal threats, although wanton terrorism remains a constant problem. However,

Table 1.5 Combat Aircraft and Tanks in GCC States

Country	Combat Aircraft		Tanks	
	1984-5	On Order	1984-5	On Order
Bahrain	–	–	–	–
Kuwait	49	24 (Mirage)	240	Scorpion
Oman	52	–	18[a]	15 (Chieftain)
Qatar	11	–	24	–
Saudi Arabia	203	5 (F-5E)[b]	450	100 (M-60A3)
United Arab Emirates	43	18 (Mirage)	178[c]	38 (Mostly Scorpion)

[a]Estimated.

[b]Saudi Arabia signed a major arms sales agreement with England in September 1985 to buy 132 Tornado combat aircraft.

[c]Includes 60 Scorpion light tanks.

Source: *The Military Balance 1984-1985* (London: International Institute for Strategic Studies, 1984), pp. 59-60, 65, 68-69, 72.

Table 1.6 Military Manpower in GCC States (1984-85)

Country	Army	Navy	Air Force	Total
Bahrain	2,300	300	200	2,800
Kuwait	10,000	500	2,000	12,500
Oman	16,500	2,000	3,000	21,500[a]
Qatar	5,000	700	300	6,000
Saudi Arabia	35,000	2,500	14,000	51,500
United Arab Emirates	40,000	1,500	1,500	43,000[b]

[a]Including some 3,700 foreign personnel.

[b]Including some 14,000 foreign personnel.

Source: *The Military Balance 1984-1985* (London: International Institute for Strategic Studies, 1984), pp. 59-60, 65, 68-69, 72.

they would still require foreign assistance should they face a serious regional crisis. Since the early 1980s, GCC states have perceived Iran as that major regional threat. Israel is also seen as a potential regional threat.

The members of the GCC vary significantly in their defense capability, depending of course on area, population, and resources. Accordingly, Saudi Arabia has the greatest capability, Bahrain, the smallest.

Although the security challenges facing the GCC states are examined below, suffice it to say here that the GCC's collective military capability remains modest. For example, Bahrain's total armed forces number under 3,000, and the country possesses no tanks or fighter aircraft.[40] The other states have small numbers of tanks and aircraft (Table 1.5). Furthermore, their total number of regular armed forces is under 140,000 (Table 1.6). This means that the GCC states are equipped to defend themselves against a modest threat but they would not be able to face a major military threat alone.

NOTES

1. *Cooperation Council for the Arab States of the Gulf* [Arabic] (Bahrain: Government Printing Office, 1983), p. 32.
2. Ibid.
3. Ibid., p. 33.
4. *A Special Report Regarding the Convening of the Fifth Summit of the GCC States in Kuwait* [Arabic] (Kuwait: Kuwait News Agency, November, 1984), p. 12.
5. Ibid.
6. Ibid.
7. Ibid., p. 13.
8. Ibid.
9. Ibid., p. 11.
10. *Cooperation Council*, p. 17.
11. Ibid., p. 18.
12. Ibid., p. 19.
13. Ibid.
14. Ibid., p. 20.
15. Ibid., pp. 24-25.
16. Ibid., p. 27.
17. Ibid., pp. 1-2.
18. *Cooperation Council for the Arab States of the Gulf* [Arabic] (Riyadh, Saudi Arabia: Bahr al-Ulum Press, 1981). See also *Cooperation Council*, pp. 93-98.
19. *Cooperation Council*, p. 93.
20. Ibid.
21. Ibid., pp. 57-59.
22. Ibid., p. 58.
23. Ibid., pp. 58-59.
24. Ibid., p. 59.
25. Ibid., pp. 99-113.
26. Ibid., pp. 99-103.
27. Ibid., pp. 104-10.
28. Ibid., pp. 111-13.
29. *The Middle East and North Africa, 1984-85* (London: Europa Publications, 1984), pp. 277, 483, 587, 599, 615, and 756.

30. *Middle East Oil and Gas* (New York: Exxon Corporation, 1984), pp. 3-5.

31. Tim Niblock and Richard Lawless, eds., *Prospects for the World Oil Industry* (London: Croom Helm, 1985), pp. 42-43.

32. Ibid., 43-44.

33. Ibid., pp. 44. In 1980 the 13 refineries were distributed as follows: five in Kuwait; five in Saudi Arabia; one in Bahrain; one in Qatar; and three in the United Arab Emirates.

34. Ibid. By 1986, seven new refineries would be completed in GCC countries.

35. Ibid., p. 47.

36. Ibid., pp. 49-55.

37. Ibid., pp. 58-61. See also *Middle East Oil and Gas*, pp. 38-39.

38. Ibid., p. 61.

39. Emile A. Nakhleh, *The Persian Gulf and American Policy* (New York: Praeger, 1982), pp. 8-11.

40. *The Military Balance 1984-85* (London: International Institute for Strategic Studies, 1984), pp. 59-60.

2
THE GCC AND REGIONAL COOPERATION

The primary purpose behind the establishment of the Gulf Cooperation Council has been to foster cooperation among member states, to further already existing cooperative arrangements, and to initiate new regional projects that would serve the interests of the peoples of the region. Areas of cooperation are thought to include economics, security, education, culture, development, industrial planning, and foreign policy issues.

Economic cooperation has included the following, at least in agreements and official pronouncements: trade in nationally produced goods; movement of indigenous populations, labor, professionals, and capital; protection of indigenous industries; uniform minimum tariff agreements; and coordination of regional industrial planning. Security cooperation was envisioned as including the exchange of security data, joint military exercises, coordination regarding the acquisition of military equipment and weapons systems, joint efforts to fight domestic and regional terrorism, continuous coordination to build a credible defense in the face of potential regional threats, either ideological or military, and the adoption of a unified defense posture toward the major powers.

Beyond economic and security cooperation, the GCC was perceived as a forum for cooperation in other important areas as well. These included education, information, science and technology, control of environmental, especially marine, pollution communications, agriculture, animal husbandry, and fishing. Of course, each of these areas potentially includes many subareas as well. For example, in education, GCC planners hope to cover such areas as curriculum in all stages, basic required subjects, teacher training, textbooks, laboratory equipment and audiovisual supplies, and student and teacher exchanges. Similarly, in the area of information, it is hoped that GCC states would cooperate in the production of radio and television entertainment and news programs, broadcasting hours and channels, news agencies, and movement of newspaper correspondents and representatives of news agencies.

Before we explore the many facets of cooperation in the remainder of this chapter, several observations should be made. First, present cooperative projects in the GCC states may be divided into two groups. Those projects that began prior to signing either the GCC Charter or the Unified Economic Agreement in 1981, and those initiated since the creation of the GCC. In fact, most of the major regional projects were initiated by Gulf states, including Iraq, before 1981. The following examples illustrate this history of economic agreements among Gulf states:

1. The Dry Dock was established in Bahrain in 1968 with contributions from the United Arab Emirates, Bahrain, Kuwait, Saudi Arabia, Iraq, Qatar, and Libya.
2. The Gulf International Bank was established in Bahrain in 1975 with contributions from the United Arab Emirates, Bahrain, Kuwait, Saudi Arabia, Iraq, Oman, and Qatar.
3. The Arab Maritime Company was established in Kuwait in 1976 with contributions from the United Arab Emirates, Bahrain, Kuwait, Saudi Arabia, Iraq, and Qatar.
4. The Gulf Organization for Industrial Consultancies was established in Qatar in 1976 with contributions from the United Arab Emirates, Bahrain, Kuwait, Saudi Arabia, Iraq, Oman, and Qatar.
5. The Union of Chambers of Commerce, Industry, and Agriculture for the Gulf Arab States was established in Kuwait in 1979 with contributions from the United Arab Emirates, Bahrain, Kuwait, Saudi Arabia, Iraq, Oman, and Qatar.[1]

Second, regional economic cooperation, at least as it was envisioned under the Unified Economic Agreement, has not proceeded as fast as was originally hoped. Implementation of some of the provisions in the agreement has been delayed for both economic and political reasons. This fact is particularly disturbing to proponents of regional cooperation because the original focus of the GCC founding fathers was on the economic and not the security aspects of cooperation.

Third, the slow pace of economic cooperation has affected those areas that were initially perceived as easily doable in terms of regional cooperation. These include a minimum tariff on nationally produced goods when traded among the member states and the movement of GCC citizens for professional or business purposes from one GCC country to another. Of course, more difficult issues, from oil production to noncompetitive economic projects, still await action.

Fourth, in the security sphere, regional cooperation has not progressed as rapidly as some had hoped, again perhaps for political reasons. Much publicity has been given to the joint military exercises, known as the "Desert Shield," which were held in 1983 and 1984. However, the joint exercises that were supposed to be held in November 1985 were postponed indefinitely without any explanations. It should be noted that contacts among GCC ministers of the interior intensified considerably in the face of the events of 1985 with an eye toward a collective, regional effort to combat terrorism. This was the subject of the meeting in Riyadh, Saudi Arabia, in September 1985.[2]

Fifth, regional cooperation among the GCC states has been adversely affected by the economic recession that swept those states in the early to mid-1980s and by a negative balance of payments due to a decline in both the price and production of oil. Hundreds of projects have had to be postponed, and a drastic retrenchment in programs has been initiated to alleviate this negative balance. A review of the following figures illustrates the situation.

A 1985 study by the British Westminster National Bank indicated that Saudi Arabia was expected to post an unprecedented deficit for 1985 (second only to the United States). Only four years earlier, the country enjoyed a $40 billion surplus in its balance of payments. However, by 1983, this surplus had been replaced by a deficit of $18.4 billion, and by a deficit of $12.5 billion for 1984.[3]

Another study drew a similar picture. For cxample, the total revenues of the GCC states have shown a steady decline throughout the 1980s: from $93.8 billion in 1981/82 to $83.6 billion in 1984/85 to $78.4 billion in 1985/86. The $29.9 billion surplus these countries enjoyed in 1981/82 was replaced two years later by a deficit totaling over $15 billion.[4] Disturbingly, reductions in government spending have not paralleled the reduction in revenues. Table 2.1 gives a breakdown of revenues and expenditures in the four wealthiest GCC states.

Table 2.1 Revenues and Expenditures in Four GCC States, 1981-85 (billions of dollars)

	1981		1982		1983		1984		1985	
Country	Rev.	Exp.	Rev.	Exp.	Rev.	Exp.	Rev.	Exp.	Rev.	Exp.
Saudi Arabia	107.7	83.3	71.7	70.9	64.4	74.4	60.2	72.5	55.4	NA*
Kuwait	15.4	13.5	11.07	10.7	10.4	12.7	10.6	13.0	10.4	12.5
United Arab Emirates	6.3	5.6	4.4	5.2	3.5	5.01	3.5	4.7	3.5	4.0
Qatar	5.2	4.06	4.5	4.2	2.4	3.9	3.3	4.6	2.7	4.7

*Not available but expected to be very high.
Source: *Al-Watan*, August 17, 1985, p. 6.

ECONOMIC COOPERATION: THE UNIFIED ECONOMIC AGREEMENT

As was stated previously, economic cooperation among the Gulf states dates back many years prior to the founding of the Gulf Cooperation Council. However, since one of the primary goals of the GCC is to foster and enhance economic cooperation, it was decided at the inception of the organization that a formal agreement would be concluded to provide a basis for economic cooperation. Broadly, such an agreement was perceived to be a tool to facilitate the economic and professional mobility of GCC nationals and to support the production and marketing of goods and commodities by GCC companies and manufacturing enterprises.

Less than three weeks after the Charter was adopted, the Gulf Cooperation Council drafted an agreement that defined the parameters for economic cooperation among the member states. The resulting Unified Economic Agreement was approved in principle on June 8, 1981 and was formally ratified by the GCC heads of state at their summit in November 1981. Of course, the agreement had to be approved by individual member states according to their respective internal political processes. It was formally ratified by member states on the following dates: Bahrain, December 26, 1981; United Arab Emirates, April 10, 1982; Saudi Arabia, April 18, 1982; Qatar, May 24, 1982; Oman, July 8, 1982; and Kuwait, November 1, 1982.[5] During the third summit (Bahrain, November 9-11, 1982), the GCC heads of states decided to begin gradual implementation of the agreement, starting March 1, 1983.

The Unified Economic Agreement consists of a preamble and seven chapters divided into a total of 28 articles.[6] Chapter topics are as follows:

1. Trade exchange (Articles 1-7).
2. Movement of capital and citizens and exercise of economic activities (Articles 8-9).
3. Coordination of development (Articles 10-13).
4. Technical cooperation (Articles 14-17).
5. Transport and communication (Articles 18-20).
6. Financial and monetary cooperation (Articles 21-23).
7. Closing provisions (Articles 24-28).

In order to "coordinate and unify their economic, financial and monetary policies, as well as their commercial and industrial legislation" (Preamble), member states had to devise ways to encourage the production and transportation of GCC-produced goods. These goods include "all agricultural, animal, industrial and natural resource products" (Article 1).

According to Article 3, to qualify for "national origin," a product must pass two tests: (a) the value added to the product during the manufacturing stage in GCC member states shall not be less than 40 percent of the final value; and (b) at least 51 percent of the manufacturing plant must be owned by GCC citizens, either from one country or a combination of countries. Also, products of a national origin must be accompanied by a "certificate of origin" signed by the appropriate officials of the country where the item was produced. GCC-produced goods will be "exempted from customs and duties and other charges having equivalent effect" (Article 4). Secondly, by adopting "a uniform minimum customs tariff regarding products of third countries" (Article 4), national products would be protected from foreign competition.

The demand for a certificate of national origin has been criticized by some local business people. In a newspaper interview following the implementation of this provision of the agreement on September 1, 1985, the executive director of the Bahrain Aluminum Sheets Company, Abd al-Mun'im Muhammad Qasim al-Shirawi, objected to the certificate of national origin on grounds of confidentiality.[7] He maintained that the information demanded in the certificate includes highly sensitive company secrets that should not be revealed lightly. Furthermore, Mr. al-Shirawi stated that it would be very difficult to itemize the product's final value, which includes such variables as the original value, manufacturing costs, marketing and advertising expenses, and suggested sale price. Also these variables can be influenced by market conditions and by the psychological attitudes of customers.[8]

Article 7 of the agreement identifies four specific objectives that would serve the larger goal of a harmonious trade balance among the GCC states: (a) to coordinate the regulation of exports and imports, (b) to coordinate policies regarding stockpiling strategic food items, (c) to conclude collective economic agreements when such agreements would serve the mutual interests of the member states, and (d) to create a GCC collective negotiating force to deal with third parties that have export/import relations with GCC countries. The fourth objective applies principally to negotiations with international and regional organizations such as the European Economic Community (EEC). Indeed, the only substantive negotiations along these lines have been held with the EEC to convince EEC countries to reduce their tariffs on GCC petrochemical products from the present level of 13-14 percent. GCC officials have indicated that if no agreement is reached with the EEC, their countries would retaliate by raising their tariffs on EEC exports to GCC countries. These exports are estimated at $20-30 billion annually.[9]

In order to encourage GCC citizens to expand their economic and professional activities throughout the GCC states, Article 8 of the Unified Economic Agreement enjoins GCC member states from discriminating against the citizens of other member states. Equal treatment of GCC citizens applies to the following areas: (a) freedom of movement, work, and residence, (b) right of ownership, inheritance, and bequest, (c) freedom of economic activity, and (d) the free movement of capital. Since the adoption of the agreement, individual GCC states have implemented legislation clarifying certain provisions in Article 8. For example, all member states have identified the following professions as being an economic activity falling under the definition of Article 8: (a) medicine, (b) law, (c) accounting, (d) engineering, and (e) consultancies in administrative, economic, technical, agricultural, fishing, and industrial fields. GCC citizens who wish to practice these professions, either individually or in conjunction with other GCC citizens, or who wish to open offices for the practice of these professions in other GCC countries must register with the proper authorities. Concerning the establishment of new companies by GCC citizens, the member states have adopted legislation allowing other GCC citizens to form such companies. However, a five-year transitional period has been built into the legislation so that at least 25 percent of the stock of companies founded from 1983 to 1988 must be owned by citizens of the host country.

Chapter 3 (Articles 10-13) focuses on coordination in development and planning, particularly in oil, with some attention paid to other industrial planning. Coordination in the oil sector would also involve the production, refining, marketing, processing, pricing, and exploitation of natural gas (Article 11). This coordination would also apply to the oil policy of GCC countries vis-à-vis regional and international organizations.

The agreement specified three steps to be taken by GCC countries in order to achieve cooperation in the industrial sector: (a) coordination of industrial activities and policies, particularly in the area of industrial diversification, (b) standardization of industrial legislation and regulations, and (c) allocation of industries among member states according to feasibility and economic benefit (Article 12). Member states were also urged to establish "joint ventures in the fields of industry, agriculture and services" (Article 13). Such ventures would be funded by capital from both the public and private sectors.

In terms of economic cooperation, Articles 10-13 are the crux of the Unified Economic Agreement. Unfortunately, it is also in this area that cooperation has been least evident. In a press conference (August 1985), the Kuwaiti Minister of Economics and Finance, Jasim al-Khurafi, indicated that the results of economic cooperation in the context of the GCC have not matched expectations. He also inferred that lack of agreement within OPEC has had negative effects on the revenues of the producing countries and in turn on regional economic cooperation.[10] On the other hand, the Qatari Director of the Technical Center for Economic Development, Said al-Mishal, has emphasized the need for a comprehensive industrial development strategy if the GCC states hope to protect and nurture their national industries. He also indicated that a draft paper on strategies of economic development was prepared for review by the GCC's Committee of Scientific and Technological Cooperation. Among the topics discussed in the draft paper were the nature of economic development strategies, general objectives of economic development, options for industrialization, industrial incentives, issues relating to technology transfers, modalities of implementation, and the labor force.[11]

GCC businessmen and industrialists have often argued that if regional economic cooperation is to become a reality, national industries must be protected from foreign competition and must be given special treatment within the GCC states. Indeed, this topic was the main item on the agenda of the first conference of GCC industrialists (Doha, Qatar, fall 1985).[12] The same theme was reiterated in another press interview with a Bahraini industrialist who said that economic cooperation must be "comprehensive."[13] He proposed that no license should be given to a new industry if a similar one already exists in any GCC country. The other major problem is the availability of foreign goods on GCC markets at prices that make it extremely difficult for indigenous industries to compete.[14]

Technical cooperation is defined under chapter four of the agreement (Articles 14-17). Member states are urged to find "spheres for common technical cooperation," to support research in applied sciences and technology, and to adapt imported technology to the needs of the region (Article 14). Member states are also urged to develop uniform regulations covering technology transfer through agreements with foreign governments and scientific and technological firms (Article 15). In addition, policies toward vocational and professional training should be coordinated. Such training programs should also be linked to the educational curricula of the respective member states (Article 16). Manpower policies and occupational classifications should be similarly coordinated among the member states (Article 17).

Manpower seems to be the predominant issue in most of the literature on economic development and industrial planning in the Gulf. Indeed, manpower planning is perhaps the primary challenge facing policymakers in the GCC. There is a feeling of apprehension in GCC countries about the long-term impact of the presence of millions of foreign workers on Gulf societies, particularly since a significant percentage of these workers are now non-Arab and non-Sunni Moslems. To illustrate this point, a recent study by the Arab League has estimated the number of Arab workers in Gulf countries, including Iraq, at approximately 4 million (1983). The vast majority of these workers were Egyptians. However, it was also estimated that the number of non-Arab workers (from India, Pakistan, Bangladesh, Iran, South Korea, Philippines, Thailand, and Sri Lanka) would reach 1.2 million by 1985, which amounts to 35 percent of the total foreign labor force. The dramatic rise in the numbers of Southeast Asian workers has forced governments to pay serious attention to the problem of foreign manpower.[15]

This problem has become even more acute because of the recent economic recession in the oil countries and the resulting retrenchment policies. GCC officials have finally begun to discuss the need for a comprehensive regional manpower policy openly. In an interview,

Bahrain's minister of labor and social affairs, Shaikh Khalifa bin Sulman bin Muhammad al-Khalifa, identified labor and manpower training as two major issues facing the GCC. He stated that the long-term goal of the GCC is to ensure that the bulk of the labor force be indigenous. The minister also revealed that draft agreements are being prepared regarding the establishment of joint manpower training centers in GCC countries.[16] However, the record indicates that the minister's optimism is not shared by other GCC officials. In fact, the percentage of indigenous manpower as compared to the total labor force has decreased dramatically in recent years. In Kuwait, for example, the percentage of indigenous labor in the country dropped from 30 percent in 1975 to 19.2 percent in 1985.[17]

The Kuwaiti executive director of the Public Agency for Training and Applied Education, Isa al-Rifa'i, described the situation as very serious. He said that the drop in the percentage of indigenous labor has occurred in spite of the fact that Kuwait has several vocational training centers, a university, and large numbers of students overseas. Despite these attempts, al-Rifa'i stated that ample employment opportunities seemed to be available to foreign, particularly Asian, labor.[18]

The Unified Economic Agreement also calls on the member states to cooperate in the fields of land, sea, and air transportation infrastructures such as seaports, airports, and roads (Article 19). This cooperation also extends to communications and related infrastructures such as power stations. In addition, ships and cargoes of member states must be accorded equal rights and privileges. Such privileges shall apply to "fees, loading and unloading, maintenance, repair, and storage of goods" (Article 20).

Cooperation under the agreement also extends to financial and monetary policy. This includes a common investment policy (Article 21), a coordinated banking policy, including the establishment of a GCC currency (Article 22), and a unified approach to regional and international aid for development (Article 23). Very little cooperation has actually occurred in this area; member states guard their financial prerogatives jealously. Secondly, GCC states have different often diametrically opposed approaches to the investment of their capital in foreign financial institutions. Neither have GCC countries been able to agree on any one approach to foreign aid.

Numerous decisions have been taken by the GCC member states, collectively and individually, since November 1981 to implement the different provisions of the Unified Economic Agreement. Dozens of meetings of government officials have been held to draw up agreements for the implementation of the agreement. These officials have represented numerous ministries, agencies, and departments in their own governments. Some of these departments are commerce; census and statistics; agriculture; finance; justice; planning; transportation and communications; civil service; electricity and water; archaeology and museums; standards, weights, and measurements; and oil. Of course, representatives of other agencies that fall outside the scope of economic cooperation, such as security, foreign policy, and information, have also met frequently.[19]

The purpose of most meetings immediately after the adoption of the Unified Economic Agreement was to create the necessary structure for economic cooperation, to urge the member states to adopt the necessary legislation for cooperation, and to define and amplify some articles in the agreement. For example, on this last point, nationally produced goods that would be exempted from tariffs in GCC countries include the following: crushed stone, metals, engine oil, soda drinks, insulation sheets, powder detergents, steel rods for construction, tobacco and dried lemon, paper bags and cardboard boxes, aluminum products, air conditioners, paper napkins, asphalt, steel pipes and plastic sheets.[20]

At the third GCC summit (Bahrain, November 1982), the Supreme Council approved the adoption of the following steps:

1. To exempt all agricultural, animal, industrial, and natural resource products of national origin from customs duties or tariffs.
2. To accord all means of national transport rights in each GCC country equal to the rights given to domestic transport institutions.
3. To facilitate the transit of goods among member states.
4. To guarantee freedom of economic activity by citizens of any GCC country in other GCC countries. Approved activities include animal husbandry, agriculture, industry, fishing, contracting, hotels and restaurants, medicine, law, accounting, engineering, consultancy, pharmaceuticals, and handicrafts of all types.[21]

In response to the action of the Supreme Council, each of the member states initiated legislation to formalize the process in accordance with the Unified Economic Agreement. Such legislation also considered the recommendations of GCC standing committees. For example, at its fifth meeting (Riyadh, Saudi Arabia, May 1983), the Committee for Economic and Financial Cooperation recommended that beginning in September 1983, a minimum tariff of 20 percent be levied on products of third countries. This recommendation was approved by the Ministerial Council in the same month.[22] Member states were given the right to set up their own schedule for the adoption of this recommendation if the September 1, 1983 deadline proved difficult to meet. However, all member states were able to implement the minimum tariff on the recommended date. In addition, countries other than Bahrain, which already collects a minimum of 5 percent on goods of third countries, had to raise their minimum tariff to meet the 4 percent requirement.

In order to institutionalize economic cooperation in light of the agreement, the GCC Supreme Council approved in 1983 the establishment of two new regional structures: the Agency for Standards and Measurements and the Gulf Investment Corporation.[23]

Since 1983, the GCC and its specialized committees have been very active in promoting economic and technical cooperation among the member states and in resolving some of the issues that have hindered cooperation. Some of these activities have been highly successful; others have not. The successes may be attributed to the fact that much of this cooperation has focused on functional issues with a low political content. Also, much of the activity is still in the research stage. In interviews Gulf officials blend optimism and caution. They are optimistic about the potential and cautious about the factors, political and economic, that might impede cooperation. There is a consensus among them that the GCC has accomplished a great deal but that much remains to be done.

In an interview Khalil Ibrahim al-Mutawwa', director of customs in Bahrain, said that for economic cooperation to function effectively, two cardinal principles must be observed: (1) competition on an equal footing, and (2) uniformity of state support. He said the most urgent need is to agree on and enforce a unified minimum tariff. Of course, some goods are excepted but these should be very few. Support of local industries by GCC states may be accomplished by the following: elimination of tariffs; protection of indigenous industries; and use of locally produced products.

Al-Mutawwa' also provided some statistical evidence that GCC citizens have already begun trading activity under the agreement. As an example, consider the activity between Bahrain and other GCC countries under the Unified Economic Agreement. Between March 1 and December 31, 1983, Bahrain imported goods valued at 10.1 million Bahraini dinars ($30.3 million). During the same period, it exported to other GCC countries goods valued at 9.5 Bahraini dinars ($28.5 million). For the first half of 1984 (January 1-June 30), Bahraini exports to other GCC countries under the Unified Economic Agreement totaled 9.8 million Bahraini dinars ($29.4 million). Over half of these exports were in aluminum products. Bahraini imports from GCC countries during that period totaled almost 4 million Bahraini dinars ($12 million).[24]

Similar themes were raised in an interview with the Bahraini deputy assistant secretary of finance, Rashid al-Mir. He maintained that smooth economic cooperation requires the GCC to respond to four immediate needs: (1) coordination of tariffs; (2) agreement on state subsidies to local industries; (3) elimination of competition and duplication; and (4) an agreement on marketing goods of local origin internationally. Al-Mir identified five major constraints on economic development: manpower; education and training; uneven incomes; legal constraints; and bureaucracy. Because of the "organic link" between economics and politics, al-Mir argued that economic cooperation will always be influenced, positively and negatively, by existing political realities, both within the countries themselves and in the region as a whole.[25]

Cooperation has also been slow in the area of water and electricity. More comprehensive coordination is required in this area according to Jamil Alawi, deputy minister of public works, electricity and water in Bahrain. He indicated that six GCC committees have been set up to deal with water and electricity, each of which is headed by a deputy minister. They are committees for power connections; training in water and electricity; unification of measurements and specifications of electrical and water instruments; exchange of data; operations and maintenance; and conservation.

According to Alawi, several needs must be addressed:

1. A comprehensive survey of the needs of GCC countries in water and electricity. Since advanced technology in this area is expensive, coordination becomes essential.
2. Training programs and centers, particularly in light of the shortage of indigenous manpower.
3. Unification of measurements, specifications and standards for materials, equipment and instruments.
4. Exchange of data.
5. Operations and maintenance.

The long-range goal is to establish a regional power grid accompanied by unification of the systems of operations and maintenance, wholesale purchasing of equipment and encouragement of Gulf industries in this area.[26]

Another high-level Bahraini official admitted that the implementation of decisions and resolutions remains a major problem in the GCC. He cited the Weights and Standards Agency as a case in point. The GCC states need to unify their measurements and weights standards, yet they have not emulated the model agency that exists in Saudi Arabia. The same point applies to food. He noted that although food security is fundamental, no GCC strategy has been developed to address this problem.[27] Most of the officials interviewed agreed that in the absence of effective regional agreements, individual bilateral relations would continue to play an important role.

By late 1985, more and more plans had begun to develop along the lines of regional economic integration. In one statement, the executive director of the Gulf Organization for Industrial Consultancies, Dr. Abdallah al-Mi'jil, revealed that serious attempts are being made by GCC states to diversify their productive base and to create a "balanced and economically productive structure" within the GCC.[28] The industrial underpinning of such a structure, Dr. al-Mi'jil maintained, would consist of petrochemicals, iron and steel, cement, and bricks. Furthermore, the balance within the prospective industrial structure would be maintained through economic complementarity, not competition.

Although economic cooperation is the cornerstone of the Unified Economic Agreement, GCC states have made significant attempts at integration in such other areas as education, agriculture, and information.

Cooperation in education has been frequently cited as a major goal of the Council. However, it is interesting to note that the first meeting ever of the GCC ministers of education was not held until September 1985. One should hasten to add that educational cooperation has taken place under the auspices of the Arab Education Office of the Gulf states, which has been in existence for several years and which also includes Iraq. Indeed, in a recent interview, Bahrain's education minister attributed the apparent slow pace of educational cooperation under the GCC to two factors: First, significant educational cooperation existed even before the creation of the GCC; second, GCC policymakers have directed their attention to more immediate issues such as economic and industrial planning and security.[29] In fact, the eighth annual conference of the Gulf Arab states' education ministers

(Qatar, March 1985) was concerned with matters relating to educational, scientific, and cultural coordination among the Arab states of the Gulf.[30]

In an interview, Bahrain's deputy minister of education, Hamad al-Sulayti, said that the thrust of educational cooperation is twofold: the Gulf Arab University (Bahrain) and curricular planning. Policy planners in this area are guided by two goals: to avoid duplication of efforts; and to define the common attitudes and culture that would enrich the school curriculum. He identified four immediate needs: studies; surveys; common syllabi; and coordination in the scientific and technical fields. He noted that in 1985 discussions were held on three topics: a master textbook; common textbooks; and a plan for common texts in math. The main problem facing educational cooperation, according to al-Sulayti, is the "uneven level of educational development in different GCC countries."[31] He also stated that agreement had been reached within the GCC on a statement defining the general educational goals for curricula in the Gulf Arab states. The 1983 draft of this statement, which follows below, was prepared by the Arab Education Office of the Gulf states. It has become the basis for educational coordination among GCC states.

1. The GCC states have agreed to cooperate in curricular development, at least on the general foundations of curricula. Three foundations were delineated: psychological; social; and educational.

2. Gulf cooperation in education is natural because of the common characteristics among the GCC states: common geography, natural resources (oil), religion (Islam), language (Arabic) and culture (tribal).

3. Social foundations for educational cooperation include the following:

a. The Gulf states are basically Islamic societies which believe in Islam as a religion and a way of life.

b. Gulf states are part of the Arab nation.

c. Gulf societies are experiencing very rapid change and in spite of their fast development, they still suffer from aspects of underdevelopment: high illiteracy and a shortage of technically trained manpower.

d. The Gulf is a very important region—economically and geographically.[32]

At the conclusion of their meeting (Riyadh, Saudi Arabia, September 10-11, 1985), the GCC ministers of education adopted the following general policies regarding education:

1. Teaching is a specialized vocation, and only those who are highly qualified should be employed in it.

2. Illiteracy must be completely eradicated from the GCC states.

3. Higher education at the university level must be Arabized in all of its disciplines and branches.

4. Citizenship, obedience, and the ability to defend one's homeland should also be nurtured through military education in schools.[33]

The ministers of education also adopted the following resolutions:

1. A minimum level of basic education must be provided for all (elementary and middle education).

2. Creativity, independent thinking, and analytical reasoning must be encouraged in schools.

3. Educational curricula and textbooks must be unified throughout the GCC states.

4. Special education must be encouraged. Educational opportunity must also be made available to the disabled.

5. Higher education must respond to society's needs and must train enough future leaders.

6. Scientific research must be employed to solve the society's problems and its capabilities must be utilized without excessive reliance on imported technology.

7. General principles for higher education must be laid down, and they must reflect the Arab and Islamic heritage of Gulf societies.[34]

In the area of agriculture the GCC has taken some steps to promote regional cooperation. At their second meeting (Qatar, January 1984), the GCC ministers of agriculture approved a long-range program aiming at achieving self-sufficiency in agriculture. The program called for self-sufficiency in vegetable, fruit, fish products, and poultry.[35] The United Arab Emirates' minister of agriculture, Said al-Raqbani, stated (August 1985) that coordination in agriculture and fishing is already a reality.[36]

A recent study of agricultural self-sufficiency predicted that by the year 2000 most GCC states will definitely be on their way toward self-sufficiency in agricultural products (Table 2.2). Another recent study by the federation of the GCC Chambers of Commerce, Industry, and Agriculture described the problem of food security as desperate and recommended that:

1. More land be reclaimed.

2. The use of scientific methods in agriculture, such as plastic agriculture and drip irrigation, be expanded.

Table 2.2 Agricultural Self-Sufficiency of GCC States by Year 2000 (percentage of self-sufficiency)

Country	Corn	Fish	White Meats	Red Meats	Eggs	Dairy Products	Oils
Saudi Arabia	98	48	82	5	87	29	12
United Arab Emirates	100	95	NA	NA	NA	NA	NA
Oman	NA	98	85	28	85	24	NA
Kuwait	NA	NA	88	NA	82	11	NA
Bahrain	NA	NA	62	6.2	65	20	NA

NA = information is not available.
Source: *Al-Qabas,* August 15, 1985, p. 4.

3. Local fertilizer and insecticides industries be established.
4. More fisheries be developed.
5. Dairy, egg, and chicken production be expanded.[37]

In a related development, the GCC reported that it was studying a plan that calls for the establishment of veterinary labs to diagnose horse diseases and to develop the proper antidotes.[38]

Information is another area that has been the subject of cooperative arrangements among GCC states. Cooperation has involved news agencies, radio programs, and even the creation of a regional GCC radio program, called the "Voice of the Gulf Cooperation Council." This program, initiated in July 1985, would broadcast from Abu Dhabi for three months and then would rotate among the GCC states at three-month intervals. The "Voice" would be heard two hours daily.[39]

In the spring of 1984, the GCC called on member states to assist their national news agencies in obtaining current information. GCC officials stressed the need for objective political analysis of the news and recommended that ARABSAT be used to serve Gulf news agencies.[40]

At their first meeting (October 1985), the GCC ministers of information discussed a draft agreement on further cooperation. The agreement, which consists of eleven articles, aims at strengthening the cooperation in the field of information, especially as it pertains to radio and television programs and news. The information ministers also discussed three working papers regarding the state of cooperation in information, the nature of joint information action, and the methods to be used to effect more and better cooperation in the field of information.[41]

SECURITY COOPERATION

Like economic cooperation, security coordination in one form or another had existed among Gulf Arab states for many years prior to the formation of the Gulf Cooperation Council. As a regional organization, however, the GCC clearly attempted to strengthen and facilitate the coordination of security among the member states. Under the auspices of the GCC, security cooperation in the 1980s has been concentrated in three discrete but related areas: domestic, regional, and international. Of course, not all efforts at security cooperation have been successful; success depended on the crisis, the time, and the capability of the actors.

Domestically, GCC security cooperation has consisted of an exchange of data on the presence and activities of expatriates–individuals, workers, and organizations–in member countries and on the political, ideological, and religious orientations of present and potential opponents of the regimes. In recent years, target populations have included Iranian nationals, pro-Iranian indigenous Shi'ites, Sunni fundamentalists, Palestinian radicals, indigenous reform-oriented intellectuals critical of current policy, and any of the underground organizations and fronts, either of recent vintage or dating back to the 1960s and 1970s. Surveillance data, particularly as concerns travel, are exchanged among the member states almost routinely. It is believed that the anti-regime plot in Bahrain in December 1981 was uncovered due to passport-related information received from another Gulf state about one of the principals in that plot.

Regionally, security cooperation among the GCC states extends to organizing joint military exercises, exchanges of military information about troops and training, coordinating a common position toward the Iraq-Iran war and its concomitant Iranian threat, discussing the impact of the Palestinian conflict on inter-Arab politics, and assessing the threat to shipping in the Gulf, particularly through the Strait of Hormuz. As the Iraq-Iran war enters its sixth year, the GCC has realized that the longer it lasts, the greater the danger for all member states, regardless of who ultimately emerges victorious. Should hostilities be extended to the combatants' oil facilities, causing Iran's oil exports from Kharg Island and elsewhere to be interrupted, the probability of Iranian retaliation in the Gulf would increase dramatically. Indeed, the Iraqi air strikes against Iran's principal oil terminal at Kharg Island in September 1985 forced GCC states to examine scenarios involving potential military retaliation by Iran. Other states, including the United States, also began to evaluate the threat of an Iranian retaliation against targets on the Arab side of the Gulf.[42]

On the international level, GCC security cooperation includes attempts to establish a common position on arms purchases from major powers, particularly as pertains to the three main sources of weapons: the United States, Western Europe, and the Soviet Union. GCC countries are extremely interested in coordinating their arms purchases in order to develop functional compatibility of their weapons systems—a necessary requirement for joint military exercises.

The United States has to date been the primary supplier of sophisticated weapons to GCC states, especially to Saudi Arabia. In addition to the American F15s and F16s, these states have purchased combat jets from England (Tornados) and from France (Mirage 2000s). Although they have frequently stated their desire to buy principally from the United States, GCC states have often been frustrated by the fact that their requests for sophisticated weapons are invariably delayed by domestic political considerations in the United States. These constraints are usually applied by supporters of Israel in the United States Congress who often argue that such arms sales are inimical to Israeli regional security. Consequently some GCC countries have sought other suppliers. For example, Kuwait signed an arms agreement with the Soviet Union in 1984 for approximately $300 million. It was the Soviet Union's first major arms sale to any GCC state, and it is certain to have significant political ramifications in the region. However, the vast majority of GCC arms purchases still come from the West.

The second example involves Saudi Arabia. As a reaction to congressional opposition to the Reagan administration's plan to sell advanced aircraft to the Saudis, the Kingdom concluded an agreement with the British government in September 1985 for the purchase of 132 British-made Tornado combat jets, the largest single purchase order in the history of British military aviation ($4.5 billion).[43]

In addition to coordinating their policies of arms purchases, GCC countries have attempted to coordinate their foreign and defense policies toward the outside world, particularly toward the superpowers. They have agreed on some issues, but they have disagreed on many others. On the whole, lack of success in this area may be attributed to several causes.

1. From the beginning, individual GCC states have been free to conclude their own defense and foreign policy agreements with outside powers. Although one of the guiding principles of the GCC's foreign and defense policy has been to assume the sole responsibility of defending the region and therefore to exclude foreign forces from

the Gulf in 1981, Oman concluded a defense treaty with the United States that permits American troops from the U.S. Central Command to be stationed on Omani soil in times of emergency. Bahrain still provides port facilities for a small U.S. naval force, formerly known as Command Middle East Force. Saudi Arabia and the United States have maintained close and complex relations under the United States -Saudi economic and security commissions which have brought thousands of American military and defense-related personnel to Saudi Arabia.

2. GCC states have had different views on neutrality and relations with the superpowers. For example, until September 1985, Kuwait was the only GCC state that maintained diplomatic relations with the Soviet Union. It has consistently argued that neutrality by definition involves maintaining relations with both superpowers. To Saudi Arabia and the other five states, neutrality is not necessarily jeopardized by having diplomatic relations with only the United States and not the Soviet Union. The superpowers themselves, however, have not been neutral on this issue. U.S. foreign policy, for example, has been predicated upon keeping the Gulf out of the Soviet orbit and preventing any rapprochement between the Soviet Union and the Arab oil-producing states. Since the adoption of the National Security Study Memorandum on the Gulf (NSSM 238) in 1972, the U.S. government has worked actively to keep Soviet interests and presence away from the Gulf. This policy has been reaffirmed by successive U.S. administrations. This was particularly noticeable following the Soviet invasion of Afghanistan in 1979. That reaffirmation, known as the Carter Doctrine, stated that the Gulf was of vital importance to the United States, a position that has also been taken by the Reagan administration. The previously mentioned U.S.-Omani military cooperation evolved in the context of this policy. This is one reason why the United States supported the establishment of the GCC. It believed that this organization would contribute to regional security by maintaining strong friendly relations with the United States.[44]

The Soviet Union, on the other hand, has very actively sought to establish bilateral relations with the GCC states. Of course, the Soviet Union has had strong relations with Iraq and has been Iraq's major supplier of arms for years. Recent Soviet attempts to play a more active diplomatic role in the region have included visits by Soviet officials to some GCC states and frequent meetings with Gulf officials, both in the region and elsewhere. The Soviet Union has been keenly interested in reestablishing diplomatic relations with Saudi Arabia where relations have been severed for several decades. Most observers believe that it will be only a matter of time before such relations are reestablished.

A significant Soviet breakthrough in this area came with Moscow's surprise announcement on September 26, 1985 that the Soviet Union and the Sultanate of Oman had agreed to establish diplomatic relations. Since it was a strong ally of the United States, second only to Saudi Arabia in the Gulf, Oman's new diplomatic relations with the Soviet Union would seem to represent a major setback for U.S. policy in the Gulf. U.S. State Department officials were "caught off guard by this unexpected development."[45] This change is particularly interesting since Oman has been the most vocal supporter of the United States within the GCC, has invited U.S. military forces to use its ports and air fields, has supported the Washington-sponsored Camp David accords and the Egyptian-Israeli rapprochement, and has for years fought Soviet-supported rebels on its border with Marxist South Yemen (the People's Democratic Republic of Yemen).

Furthermore, it might be possible that other GCC states would be influenced by the Omani move, which of course would represent a real coup for Soviet diplomacy. Indeed, in a recent press interview, the prime minister of Bahrain, Shaikh Khalifa bin Sulman al-Khalifa, called on the GCC to establish diplomatic relations with the Soviet Union. He agreed that such a step was necessary if the GCC is to play a more active role in regional and international politics.[46] Should this occur, Washington would have to come to terms with the Kuwaiti argument that neutrality does involve having diplomatic relations with both superpowers. Such a development need not diminish United States-GCC cooperation nor should it be confrontational.[47]

3. The third reason for the lack of success in coordinating a common GCC foreign policy involves the member states' differing views on the Palestine conflict and on the modalities for resolving that conflict. Although most of them see the Palestine conflict from a triangular perspective involving the Palestinians, the Gulf, and the United States, they disagree on the approach to conflict resolution. The American side of the triangle is governed by two essential elements: The United States' special relationship with Israel and the United States' strategic and economic interests in the Gulf. Moreover, all GCC states believe, rightly or wrongly, that the United States is the only country that can bring about a peaceful resolution of the Palestinian-Israeli conflict. However, they disagree on the nature of the U.S. role. All of them agree that any peace arrangement must recognize

the legitimate rights of the Palestinian people, not necessarily an independent state, as a first step. However, they disagree on the political context in which such rights would be guaranteed. A definite sense of hesitancy characterized the GCC states' reaction to the 1985 Jordanian-PLO rapprochement. They attributed such hesitancy to Syria's objection to the agreement between Jordan's King Hussein and PLO Chairman Yasir Arafat and to dissension and internecine violence within the PLO.

Differing positions have also been evident in the GCC states' approach to violence in Lebanon, to Egypt's impending reentry into the Arab League, and to the nature of the United States' role in the peace process. The GCC states seem to believe that inter-Arab conflicts must be settled peacefully and they have campaigned actively for rapprochement among the Arab states. Some of the official visits in October and November 1983 included the following: a visit by Qatar's foreign minister to Baghdad and Damascus; a visit by the UAE president to Iraq, Syria, and Algeria; a visit by the Saudi foreign minister to Algeria; and a visit by a GCC delegation to Syria. More recently, Saudi Arabia has actively attempted to mediate the conflict between Jordan and Syria and between Syria and Iraq.

Concerning Egypt, President Husni Mubarak has made clear that his reentry into the Arab orbit would not nullify his peace treaty with Israel. GCC states seem to take this position for granted. Hussein and Arafat have also accepted the reality of Egyptian-Israeli relations. What is ironically interesting is that the Gulf states, like many other Arab states, have come to accept the three basic underpinnings of the Egyptian position on resolving the Palestinian conflict: that the conflict can only be resolved by direct negotiations between Israel and the Palestinians; that the legitimate national rights of the Palestinians must be recognized, regardless of the political arrangement; and that, to paraphrase the late President Sadat of Egypt, the United States still holds 99 percent of the cards.[48] The basic elements of GCC security policy, can be summarized in four points:

First, the security of the Gulf is the primary responsibility of its states. In exercising this responsibility, the GCC adheres to the twin principles of self-reliance and nonalignment. "GCC states believe that inviting foreign troops to protect the security of the Gulf is a formula for instability."[49]

Second, in order for GCC states to develop a credible regional defense capability, they have attempted to coordinate their military forces. The two joint military exercises held in Abu Dhabi (Desert

Shield I) and in Saudi Arabia (Desert Shield II) were an expression of this coordination. In realizing this goal, the GCC has been guided by gradualism, pragmatism, and realism.[50]

Third, Gulf security in the context of the GCC is directly equated with the continued stable existence of the present regimes and forms of government in the Gulf states. As such, the GCC is a status-quo-oriented organization and views any serious threat to the present political structure in any GCC country as a "terrorist" threat to the entire region. For example, the assassination attempt on the Kuwaiti ruler, Shaikh Jabir al-Ahmad al-Sabah, on May 25, 1985 (the fourth anniversary of the GCC) was viewed as a threat to the entire Gulf. It was also viewed as a method to "sow fear, confusion and instability in the region as a whole and in the GCC states in particular."[51] The attack was condemned by all GCC member states.[52]

Fourth, regional security is inextricably linked to internal stability. Indeed, terrorism headed the agenda of the sixth annual GCC summit (Muscat, Oman, November 1985).[53] Gulf security seems to be multidimensional and complex.[54]

The major concern of the GCC since its inception has been the continuing Iran-Iraq war; therefore member states have actively searched for a way to mediate the conflict. As early as May 1982, the UAE had announced its intention of embarking on a peace mission to end the war. In November of that same year, the king of Saudi Arabia and the deputy prime minister of Kuwait announced, on separate occasions, their serious interest in finding a resolution to the Iraq-Iran war. In August 1984, Kuwait's deputy prime minister declared at a press conference that "it was natural for the GCC states to expend every effort, either by themselves or in cooperation with other states, to stop this meaningless war."[55]

In addition to regional security, the Iraq-Iran war was another major item on the agenda of the sixth GCC summit in November 1985. On the eve of his official visit to Oman in September 1985 to prepare for the summit, the Bahraini prime minister, Shaikh Khalifa bin Sulman al-Khalifa, implored Iran to respond to mediation efforts to end the war. He also stated that the effects of this war have already been felt in other Gulf states–economically and politically.[56] At the conclusion of the sixteenth session of the GCC Ministerial Council in Riyadh, Saudi Arabia in September 1985, the foreign ministers of the six member states indicated their countries' willingness "to find a just solution" to the Iraq-Iran war. They also discussed the Iranian threats against Kuwait and examined contingency plans in the event of any military aggression against them.[57]

Many meetings have been held under the auspices of the GCC to coordinate the forces of member states. For example, the GCC's defense ministers held three meetings in August 1984 to coordinate their defense efforts. At those meetings, they reviewed the recommendations made by the GCC chiefs of staff in 1982. A joint meeting of the GCC ministers of defense and foreign affairs was held in Saudi Arabia in September 1984 to discuss the draft report prepared by the defense experts. The commanders-in-chief of the GCC also held at least five meetings prior to September 1984 (September 20, 1981; March 15, 1982; February 13, 1983; October 18, 1983; and June 23, 1984).[58]

As was stated above, the meetings resulted in two joint military exercises: Operation Desert Shield I in Abu Dhabi in October 1983 and Operation Desert Shield II in Saudi Arabia in September 1984. Bilateral military exercises have also been held in Saudi Arabia, November 1983 (Saudi Arabia and Kuwait); in Kuwait, February 1984 (Kuwait and Saudi Arabia); and in the United Arab Emirates, February 1984 (United Arab Emirates and Oman).[59]

The third GCC joint military exercises (Desert Shield III), scheduled to be held in the fall of 1985, was postponed indefinitely without explanation. However, forces from the GCC states gathered in October 1985 in Saudi Arabia for joint training and to form a joint GCC rapid deployment force.[60] Most military analysts agree that these states suffer from many impediments to effective defense. These impediments include size, geography, rivalry, and a lack of effective military planning.[61] Anthony H. Cordesman, a military expert on the Gulf, has identified ten other factors that tend to impede effective military cooperation in the GCC:

1. a lack of suitably educated personnel;
2. a rigid separation in terms of status of officers and enlisted men that prevents adequate leadership and cooperation;
3. an unwillingness on the part of officers and NCOs to become involved in training and maintenance that is regarded as "manual labor";
4. a similar lack of willingness to become involved in complex maintenance and logistic procedures;
5. chronic overcentralization of decision making and management;
6. a resulting lack of interservice cooperation and coordination;
7. a failure to operate management and administrative systems effectively;

8. nepotism and "politicization" of the promotion process;
9. overreliance on foreign assistance and advice; and
10. unwillingness to report factually on politically threatening or career-threatening readiness and force improvement problems.[62]

Perhaps the biggest disagreement among GCC states in the area of security cooperation has been over the Saudi-sponsored security agreement. Saudi Arabia began to push for it in late 1981 and early 1982, after the discovery of the destabilizing plot in Bahrain in December 1981. So far, some GCC states, particularly Kuwait, have objected strongly to the proposed agreement. In a newspaper report in May 1985, the Kuwaiti deputy prime minister emphasized his country's determination not to ratify the agreement. He said, "We will never sign any agreement that contradicts our constitution. Secondly, we will not sign the agreement before it is submitted to the National Assembly for discussion."[63]

The GCC interior ministers have held numerous meetings to discuss papers and suggestions concerning the drafting of a security agreement among the six states. The draft agreement, which has yet to be signed, contains several general principles dealing with the strengthening of security cooperation among the member states, the means to fight smuggling and crime, and the extradition of criminals. The agreement also strives for "guarding security and stability and protecting the Islamic faith from destructive, atheistic ideas and from partisan activities."[64]

Disagreements among member states over the draft security agreement were addressed at a special meeting of interior ministers held in Saudi Arabia (September 17-18, 1985). However, in a statement on the eve of that meeting, a senior government security official from Bahrain predicted that a joint GCC security agreement would be approved soon. He also denied that any reservations exist regarding this agreement.[65] At the conclusion of their meeting, the interior ministers indicated in their official communiqué that they were determined to face the new wave of terrorism that threatens their countries' security and peace. They also made three other points: Gulf security is comprehensive and indivisible. Collective security efforts must be strengthened significantly. A threat to one state is a threat to all states of the GCC; such a threat must be repelled collectively.[66]

Although a collective security agreement has yet to be signed, the GCC member states have made significant progress along the road to security cooperation in the five short years since the establishment of the GCC.

NOTES

1. Mukhtar Muhammad Mutwalli and Abd al-Mahmud Abd al-Rahman, "Economic Development in the Gulf Cooperation Council States, 1970-1982," *Journal of the Gulf and Arabian Peninsula Studies* [Arabic], vol. XI, no. 43 (July 1985), pp. 112-40.

2. *Al-Watan*, September 8, 1985, p. 7.

3. *Al-Watan*, August 24, 1985, p. 6. See also Kingdom of Saudi Arabia, *Annual Report 1404 (1984)* [Arabic] (Riyadh, Saudi Arabia: Saudi Arabian Monetary Agency, 1985).

4. *Al-Watan*, August 17, 1985, p. 6.

5. *A Special Report Regarding the Convening of the Fifth Summit of the GCC States in Kuwait* (Kuwait: Kuwait News Agency, November 1984), pp. 70-71.

6. *The Unified Economic Agreement* (Riyadh, Saudi Arabia: Gulf Cooperation Council, Secretariat, 1981).

7. *Al-Watan*, September 11, 1985, p. 7.

8. Ibid.

9. *Gulf Daily News* (Bahrain), August 8, 1985, p. 19. Quoted in *FBIS*, V, August 8, 1985, p. C1.

10. *Al-Watan* (Kuwait), August 16, 1985, p. 7.

11. Ibid.

12. Ibid.

13. *Al-Watan*, September 11, 1985, p. 7.

14. Ibid.

15. "Foreign Labor in the Countries of the GCC Countries," *Industry and Petroleum News* [Arabic] (Abu Dhabi), vol. XVI, no. 177 (April 1985), pp. 18-20.

16. A personal interview conducted December 31, 1984.

17. *Al-Watan*, July 27, 1985, p. 5.

18. Ibid.

19. *Documents of the Gulf Cooperation Council*, vol. IV (Doha, Qatar: Qatar News Agency, 1984).

20. An announcement issued by Bahrain's Department of Customs and Ports dated October 14, 1984.

21. The addition of hotels, restaurants, pharmaceuticals, and handicrafts was approved by the GCC Supreme Council at the fourth summit held in Qatar in November 1983.

22. *Gulf Cooperation Council: Initial Steps Taken by the Member States for the Implementation of the Unified Economic Agreement* [Arabic] (Riyadh, Saudi Arabia: GCC Secretariat, February 1984), p. 30.

23. Ibid., pp. 32-36.

24. A personal interview conducted December 31, 1984.

25. A personal interview conducted January 8, 1985.

26. A personal interview conducted January 6, 1985.

27. A personal interview conducted with Hasan al-Nisf, deputy minister of commerce, January 6, 1985.

28. *Al-Qabas*, August 20, 1985, p. 7.

29. A personal interview conducted January 2, 1985.

30. *Qatar News* (Washington, DC: Embassy of Qatar), vol. XII, no. 2 (March/April 1985), pp. 4-5.

31. A personal interview conducted January 7, 1985.

32. Obtained from the office of Bahrain's minister of education, January 2, 1985.

33. *Al-Qabas*, September 13, 1985, p. 4.

34. A statement by Dr. Hasan al-Ibrahim, Kuwait's minister of education, upon his return from the first conference of the GCC ministers of education in ibid.

35. *Qatar News* (Washington, DC: Embassy of Qatar), vol. XII, no. 1 (January/February 1984), pp. 3-4.

36. *Al-Watan*, August 11, 1985, p. 7.

37. *Gulf Mirror* (Bahrain), August 8, 1985, p. 13. Quoted in *FBIS*, V, August 9, 1985, p. C1.

38. *Al-Watan*, May 19, 1985, p. 4.

39. *Al-Watan*, July 29, 1985, p. 17; *al-Qabas*, July 30, 1985, p. 4.

40. "GCC calls for Coordination Among Gulf News Agencies," *Saudi Press Agency* (Washington, DC: May 21, 1984), pp. 1 and 4.

41. *Al-Qabas*, August 25, 1985, p. 4.

42. David B. Ottaway, "Persian Gulf War Posing New Threat to U.S. Interests," *Washington Post*, September 27, 1985, p. A32.

43. *Washington Post*, September 27, 1985, pp. A1 and A32.

44. A personal interview with U.S. ambassador to Bahrain, conducted January 2, 1985.

45. *Washington Post*, September 27, 1985, p. A33.

46. *Al-Qabas*, July 29, 1985, p. 4.

47. Hasan Ibrahim, "The United States and the GCC: Cooperation or Confrontation?" *al-Qabas*, November 21, 1984, p. 21.

48. For an analysis of the GCC's foreign policy, see Abdallah al-Ash'al, "International Relations in the Context of the GCC," *Journal of the Gulf and Arabian Peninsula Studies* [Arabic], vol. X, no. 37 (January 1984), pp. 61-89.

49. See a presentation by the GCC secretary-general, Abdallah Bishara, at a symposium on "The Gulf and the West," held at Exeter University, Exeter, England, July 6-8, 1984.

50. Abdallah Bishara, "We Don't Need Volunteers to Protect Our House," *The Middle East* (London) (November 1983), pp. 13-17.

51. *Al-Qabas*, May 30, 1985, p. 4.

52. *Al-Qabas*, May 27, 1985, p. 5.

53. *Al-Qabas*, June 20, 1985, p. 4; *al-Watan*, June 23, 1985, p. 7.

54. Robert G. Darius et al. (eds.), *Gulf Security into the 1980s: Perceptual and Strategic Dimensions* (Stanford, CA: Hoover Institution Press, 1985), pp. 117-18.

55. *A Special Report*, p. 40.

56. *Al-Qabas*, September 8, 1985, p. 4.

57. *Al-Watan*, September 4, 1985, p. 1.

58. *A Special Report*, p. 49.

59. Ibid.

60. *Al-Qabas*, September 21, 1985, p. 3.

61. *Gulf Cooperation Council* (Washington, DC: Center for Strategic and International Studies, 1984), p. 11.

62. Anthony H. Cordesman, *The Gulf and the Search for Strategic Stability* (Boulder, CO: Westview Press, 1984), p. 490.

63. *Al-Qabas*, May 22, 1985, p. 2.

64. *A Special Report*, p. 60.

65. *Al-Qabas*, September 9, 1985, p. 4.

66. *Al-Watan*, September 19, 1985, p. 11.

3
GULF OFFICIAL VIEWS OF THE GCC

Since its establishment in May 1981, the Gulf Cooperation Council has been the subject of constant analysis by its own officials, in particular the secretary-general, by government officials such as ministers and deputy ministers of the member states, and in government publications. The GCC has also been examined by such other segments of the population as intellectual reformists and the public at large. In this chapter, the focus will be on the perceptions of government officials. The opinions of the reformists and the public will be presented in the following two chapters.

Sources of these official views include summit pronouncements, official publications, newspaper interviews, and personal interviews. These views are divided into three categories: regional security, regional cooperation, and Arab issues. The bulk of official statements have focused on security, a fact that lends credence to the general belief that the GCC is first and foremost a security arrangement. As mentioned previously, the GCC came into being in the midst of major internal and international security developments in the region. In addition, the superpowers had become increasingly interested in the area since the late 1970s.

Gulf leaders have also felt threatened from within their countries from the rise of Shi'ite Islamic fundamentalism under the tutelage of Iran. Although the threat was clearly perceived, the countries did not have a clearly defined response. In early 1981 several rulers and other high-level policymakers considered the possibility of "opening up" their ruling process by initiating some sort of popular participation in government. Two forms were presented: a consultative assembly (*majlis shura*) whose members would be appointed by the ruler or a national assembly, the majority of whose members would be elected by adult male citizens. A *majlis shura* has existed in Qatar since independence in 1971. Although the provisional constitution provides for an elected *majlis shura*, so far the ruling family and the leading clans in Qatar seem satisfied with the system. In early 1981 the King of Saudi Arabia alluded to the possibility of establishing a consultative assembly in the Kingdom; however, no such body ever came into being.

The second form, a national assembly, has existed intermittently in Kuwait; a national assembly had functioned in the country from independence in the early 1960s until it was dissolved in 1976. However, it was resurrected in 1981. In Bahrain, a national assembly was established in 1973, but it was dissolved in 1975. In both cases, the national assembly consisted of popularly elected members plus the ministers as members *ex officio*.

The plethora of official statements in 1980 and 1981 following the overthrow of the Shah and the establishment of the "Islamic republic" in Iran led some observers to believe that popular political representation in the Gulf Arab states was imminent and that its implementation was just a matter of time. Only Kuwait actually reconvened its national assembly. Saudi Arabia's promise of a consultative assembly never materialized. Qatar proceeded with its *majlis shura* unchanged. Bahrain's previously dissolved national assembly remained dormant. The United Arab Emirates continued its federative system without any representative body, and Oman continued to be ruled directly by Sultan Qabus. Frightening as the violent events of that period were to Gulf rulers, a majority of them failed to devise mechanisms of sharing power with their citizens. Instead they continued to base governmental legitimacy on tribal, Islamic, and Arab traditions. At the same time, Gulf rulers called on their peoples to stand fast with them in the face of threats—threats that were perceived as emanating from non-Arab sources.

It is in this context that the GCC was born: a regional structure that would provide the six tribal states with more strength than they possessed individually. Such an entity would provide for the collective security of the member states; provide for the economic well-being of their peoples; advance the cause of Arab unity; and preserve the cultural heritage of the member states.

Most GCC statements have focused on these themes.

REGIONAL SECURITY

In a press interview on the joint military exercises in the summer of 1985, Kuwait's minister of defense, Shaikh Salim Sabah al-Salim, stated that the "Desert Shield" exercises were a strong symbol with both political and military ramifications.[1] The "Desert Shield" exercises included units from the armed forces of the six GCC states. The defense minister reiterated the often repeated official view that military cooperation in the context of the GCC is for defensive purposes only.[2]

According to Bahrain's foreign minister, Shaikh Muhammad bin Mubarak al-Khalifa, the GCC "is not an alliance against any party."[3] In a more detailed discussion of the purposes of the GCC, the Council's secretary-general, Abdallah Bishara, stated that the GCC favored the "gulfanization" of regional security; the GCC is definitely considered a collective security agreement.[4] Because of the GCC, stated Bahrain's foreign minister, "the people of the Gulf are best suited to defend the region without any need for foreign military bases."[5] In December 1981, the president of the United Arab Emirates, Shaikh Zayed al-Nhayyan, described the Gulf Cooperation Council as "an important beginning in reinforcing cooperation among the Gulf countries so that they can defend themselves. . . ."[6] These statements were corroborated at the time by other prominent officials.[7]

Self-reliance seems to be the cornerstone of the GCC in security planning. In an interview with the London-based magazine *The Middle East* in November 1983, the GCC's secretary-general, Abdallah Bishara, said that the work of the GCC falls into three fields: economic integration; self-reliance; and security.[8] He also stated that self-reliance "requires military coordination on defense issues. It also requires the pooling of whatever potentials we have . . . and . . . our potentials and our defects, our advantages and disadvantages, merits and demerits on the defense issue."[9] This theme was reiterated by the GCC secretary-general at a conference in the summer of 1984.[10] At a press conference in Austria a year later, the GCC secretary-general again mentioned self-reliance as an important goal of the GCC. "Through self-reliance the GCC states would be able to protect their cultural tradition, to contribute to the international economy, and to participate in international organizations."[11]

In a personal interview about the GCC and Gulf security, Bahrain's foreign minister, Shaikh Muhammad bin Mubarak al-Khalifa, made several points:

1. The GCC is a culmination of cooperation that has existed for many years. It is natural for these states to cooperate–they share culture, language, interests, historical experiences, religion, political system, hopes, concerns, and aspirations.

2. The GCC's concern with security should not be considered particularly unusual when one examines the regional events of the past ten years.

3. These states have expressed the desire to defend the region themselves, to establish their own security, to keep major powers out of the region, and to help settle regional conflicts without foreign interference, realizing of course that outside powers do have specific interests in the region.

4. Security in the context of the GCC involves four topics:
    a. Information.
    b. Extradition.
    c. Standardization of forces and weapons systems.
    d. Coordination of air, sea, and land defense systems.[12]

In an interview, Bahrain's minister of information, Tareq al-Moayyed, noted that, on the question of security, the GCC, as a young organization, still suffers from a gap between its rhetoric and the reality of cooperation.[13] He made two other points. First, the GCC continues to be viewed by Gulf citizens as primarily a security organization, although it is designed to address many other issues. Second, recent terrorist events in Saudi Arabia, Kuwait, and Bahrain have, in a sense, forced the GCC to focus on security matters. Cooperation in this area, particularly in the exchange and sharing of data regarding immigration, travel, and visas, has become imperative. Yet, there have been disagreements among GCC states, particularly Kuwait and Saudi Arabia or Kuwait and Oman, on how to deal with some of these security questions.[14]

A review of official statements on the role of the GCC in Gulf security would reveal at least five themes:

First, to protect the security and safety of the region and to guarantee the stability and well-being of its peoples. According to a statement by the Saudi monarch, the GCC "works for the good of the region and does not aim at harming any party, directly or indirectly. It is not a military alliance against anyone but a regional organization to serve the interests of the region and its peoples."[15]

Second, to guarantee the collective security of the GCC member states. The Omani defense minister stated in January 1982 that "the defense of the GCC is a collective effort which means that an attack on one shall be considered an attack on all."[16]

Third, the belief that the GCC military force is defensive, not offensive. The Kuwaiti defense minister stated in January 1982 that "the defense plan of the GCC will not be directed against anyone. Instead, it will be a shield to repel any threat to the security of the Gulf."[17]

Fourth, to close any gaps that might facilitate intervention of the major powers in the region.

Fifth, the belief that the GCC military power is inseparable from the efforts, directions, and goals of the Arab world.[18]

REGIONAL COOPERATION

From the very beginning, officials have viewed the Gulf Cooperation Council as a regional organization with pragmatic goals. This means that in order for regional cooperation to function effectively under the GCC's umbrella, it must be grounded in realism. According to the GCC's secretary-general, Abdallah Bishara, the member states realized several years ago their mutual strengths and weaknesses. He identified the strengths as common political systems, ideologies, aspirations, and religious cultures. The weaknesses included disagreements over oil production, pricing and marketing, small indigenous populations, and shortages of trained manpower.[19]

The pragmatic refrain was echoed in other official statements. Bahrain's minister of information said that Bahrain views the Council as a pragmatic organization designed to address real, practical issues, ranging from security to education. He added that by avoiding grandiose and lofty goals and by focusing on practical matters, the GCC has a good chance of succeeding as a regional organization.[20]

Al-Qabas, the Kuwaiti newspaper, conducted a special interview with five Bahraini ministers about their views of the GCC; several themes emerged from their responses.[21] The minister of information, Tareq al-Moayyed, indicated the following: First, the GCC reflects a common desire on the part of Gulf rulers and peoples for cooperation. In fact, the GCC is a formal structure embodying the cooperation that has been a reality for years. Second, the GCC will not undermine extant bilateral agreements; on the contrary, it will build on them and enhance cooperation. Third, in their relations among each other, Gulf states should avoid slogans and focus on substance.[22]

The minister of development and industry, Yusif al-Shirawi, said first that the Gulf states were like small boats that cannot face the strong winds on their own. The GCC provides a means by which they can proceed safely. Second, a major challenge to these small tribal city-states is preservation of their values and traditions in an age of mega-cities and technology. The GCC could help them surmount this challenge. Third, Gulf coordination is both necessary and inevitable. The thrust of such coordination should be economic.[23]

The minister of education, the late Shaikh Abd al-Aziz al-Khalifa, said in the same interview that the Gulf University, which is being established in Bahrain, is a practical embodiment of regional cooperation. He added that educational cooperation among Gulf states is natural because of their societal similarities, and that this type of cooperation is more likely to succeed because it does not suffer from the internal disagreements that plague collective action attempts on the wider Arab scale.[24]

The former minister of health, Dr. Ali Fakhro (currently the minister of education in Bahrain), asked rhetorically whether the small, weak, and rich Gulf states could live peacefully in a world that has an economic interest in the region. In answering his question negatively, Dr. Fakhro argued that the only practical solution is for these states to unite.[25] Such unified action would of course develop gradually. Dr. Fakhro stated that the GCC is a historical necessity, particularly in the face of the intensifying interests and presence of the superpowers in the region. At the present time the GCC should remain a council of governments; it is a great achievement for the heads of these states to meet regularly to discuss issues of common concern. Coordination on a lower level would come much later.[26]

The fifth minister to be interviewed was Bahrain's minister of labor and social affairs, Shaikh Khalifa bin Sulman al-Khalifa, who expressed the following views: The establishment of the GCC was an optimistic note for the future of the region—even though it was still too early to examine the Council's program of action. The meeting of the heads of the Gulf states on a regular basis was a great achievement because for the first time these leaders could discuss common issues openly and collectively. One of the most important areas of cooperation is in manpower and the coordination needed for a joint manpower training plan. Such a plan could be developed through the GCC.[27]

These themes were reiterated by Bahrain's ministers in more recent interviews conducted by the author in 1985. For example, in a personal interview, the minister of development and industry, Yusif al-Shirawi, stated that the GCC came into being as a culmination of all the regional cooperative arrangements that had previously existed among Gulf states. He also indicated that the GCC is based on the following pillars: (1) realism, pragmatism, and economy of size; (2) gradualism; (3) interdependence; and (4) state sovereignty.[28]

Minister al-Shirawi also noted that the idea of a loose regional cooperative arrangement dates back to 1970, following the collapse of the federation talks among the nine lower Gulf amirates. According to al-Shirawi, the question then was: "Shall we follow the route of the Arab League and Arab unity or shall we follow the route of a regional arrangement?"[29] Because of the economic, security, and political realities of the region, the leaders opted for a cooperative arrangement.

In another recent interview, Dr. Ali Fakhro, currently Bahrain's minister of education, also cast his perception of the GCC in pragmatic terms. He said that the Gulf University located in Bahrain is concrete evidence of GCC cooperation. The objective of such a university is to develop "an environmental approach to knowledge," which would benefit the region.[30] Financial support through the GCC has made it possible for the Gulf University to introduce new topics into the curriculum and to initiate new programs. These programs include special education; training teachers for the handicapped; advanced technology; advanced studies in curriculum development; desert sciences; energy sciences; marine sciences; innovative medical training; problem solving; and individualized learning.[31] Fakhro also indicated that cooperation among the GCC states has already produced an agreement on common mathematics texts for the first four elementary grades.[32]

In another interview on regional cooperation, Bahrain's minister of labor and social affairs, Shaikh Khalifa bin Sulman al-Khalifa, indicated that GCC cooperation in the economic and labor fields has taken into consideration several realities: the industrial infrastructure; the social-economic infrastructure; the nature of the labor market (primarily construction); and the nature of the labor force (primarily expatriate).[33]

The minister also indicated that this cooperation has enabled the GCC member states to concentrate on the most important issue facing all of them, labor and manpower requirements. They have already recognized the need to establish joint centers for management trainees, for vocational training, and for technological skills. He felt that the frequent meetings held by the GCC ministers of labor have helped all of them identify the problems facing the member states, particularly in the area of indigenous manpower training.[34]

ARAB ISSUES

The relationship between the Gulf Cooperation Council and the Arab world at large is the issue least mentioned by Gulf officials in their frequent assessments of the GCC. Four reasons have contributed to this fact.

First, Gulf officials have made it clear from the very beginning that the GCC is a regional organization applicable only to certain Gulf states that share similar and unique characteristics.

Second, Gulf officials went to great pains to explain that the GCC is not another experiment in Arab unity, particularly in light of the failure of continuous attempts at Arab unity.

Third, Gulf officials have also explained that the GCC is not a political organization *per se* but a security and economic organization.

Fourth, as a regional organization under Article 52 of the United Nations Charter, members of the GCC maintain their own political sovereignty and independence, which means that they conduct their own separate foreign policies and oftentimes take independent positions on foreign policy issues—Arab and non-Arab.

Arab issues in this context refer to three main ones: The Palestine conflict, and by implication GCC relations with the United States; the conflict in Lebanon, and by implication GCC relations with Syria and the "confrontation" states; and the Iraq-Iran war, and by implication long-term GCC relations with Iraq and Iran. Most other Arab issues, such as Egypt's dismissal from the Arab League following its peace treaty with Israel or the dissension within the Palestine Liberation Organization (PLO), are to a large degree subsumed under those three issues. While this is not a discussion of the position taken by individual GCC states on these issues, suffice it to say that as an organization, the GCC has not officially taken a unified stand on any of these issues. Indeed, in a 1984 lecture given in London, the GCC secretary-general stated categorically that the GCC "should refrain from taking part in international power politics and should observe scrupulously nonalignment."[35] However, it should be pointed out that GCC states have frequently, if not always, voted similarly on Arab issues whenever they were raised, either in the Arab League or at the United Nations. Accordingly, GCC officials have been reluctant to espouse any specific GCC position on issues transcending the Gulf. For example, in the newspaper interview with five Bahraini ministers, cited above, no reference was made by any of them to Arab issues.[36]

Similarly, in a special newspaper interview conducted with GCC ambassadors in Morocco in August 1981, all of them discussed the

GCC in its Gulf context. They did agree that the GCC was a defensive security organization aimed at no one, and that it did not violate the charter of the Arab League.[37]

In discussing security matters and in advocating a joint Gulf military force, GCC officials made it clear over the years that the purpose of such a force would be to protect the Gulf states and the Gulf region.[38] Of course, military coordination gained added significance in official statements in 1985 because of the increase of terrorism in the region. In GCC official publications, officials have stated that in the Gulf and Arab contexts, GCC foreign policy is based on five principles:

First, peace in the Gulf region is the responsibility of the Gulf states, which object to big-power meddling in the internal affairs of the Gulf.

Second, stability in the Gulf is linked to the achievement of peace in the Middle East.

Third, peace in the Middle East cannot be achieved except through the Israeli withdrawal from all occupied Arab lands, including Jerusalem.

Fourth, a satisfactory solution to the Palestine question must ensure the legitimate rights of the Palestinian people, including the right of return to their homeland and the establishment of an independent state on their land under the leadership of the PLO, the sole legitimate representative of the Palestinian people.

Fifth, the elimination of conflicts among the Arab states and the realization of Arab cooperation are the only way for the Arab nation to shoulder its national responsibility.[39]

NOTES

1. *Al-Watan*, August 14, 1985, p. 1.
2. Ibid.
3. *Al-Adwa'* (Bahrain), May 30, 1981, p. 3.
4. *Monday Morning* (Beirut), July 20-26, 1981, pp. 20-26; translated in *Foreign Broadcasting Information Service* (*FBIS*) 5 (August 6, 1981): C 1-5.
5. *Al-Adwa'*, January 17, 1981, p. 3.
6. *FBIS* 5 (December 30, 1981): C 11.
7. Emile A. Nakhleh, *The Persian Gulf and American Policy* (New York: Praeger, 1982), pp. 54-57.
8. *The Middle East* (London) (November 1983), pp. 13-14.
9. Ibid., p. 13.
10. "Symposium on the Gulf and the West," held at Exeter University, England, July 6-8, 1984. Unpublished notes.

11. *Al-Qabas*, June 16, 1985, p. 4.
12. A personal interview conducted January 3, 1985.
13. A personal interview conducted December 29, 1984.
14. Ibid.
15. *A Special Report Regarding the Convening of the Fifth Summit of the GCC States in Kuwait* [Arabic] (Kuwait: Kuwait News Agency, November 1984), p. 47.
16. Ibid.
17. Ibid., p. 48.
18. Ibid.
19. *Akhbar al-Khaleej* (Bahrain), June 23, 1981, p. 3.
20. A personal interview conducted December 29, 1984.
21. *Al-Qabas*, April 14, 1981, p. 17.
22. Ibid.
23. Ibid.
24. Ibid.
25. Ibid.
26. Ibid.
27. Ibid.
28. A personal interview conducted January 7, 1985.
29. Ibid.
30. A personal interview conducted January 2, 1985.
31. Ibid.
32. Ibid.
33. A personal interview conducted December 31, 1984.
34. Ibid.
35. "Symposium on the Gulf and the West."
36. *Al-Qabas*, April 14, 1985, p. 17.
37. *Al-Khaleej* (United Arab Emirates), August 26, 1981, p. 13.
38. *The Middle East* (November 1983), pp. 16-17.
39. *A Special Report Regarding the Convening of the Fifth Summit of the GCC States in Kuwait* [Arabic] (Kuwait: Kuwait News Agency, November 1984), p. 35.

4
GULF REFORMIST VIEWS OF THE GCC

As was pointed out in the Introduction to this book, some of the most interesting discussions of the Gulf Cooperation Council are being carried on by a group of indigenous Gulf intellectuals as part of an informal group called *Nadwat al-Tanmiya li Duwal al-Jazira al-Arabiyya al-Muntija li al-Naft* (Development Panel for the Oil-Producing States of the Arabian Peninsula), hereinafter known as *Nadwat al-Tanmiya*.[1] It was established following the holding of two meetings and several discussions among the participants in those meetings. The first meeting, which was held in Abu Dhabi in 1979, focused on the "role of public projects in the Arab oil producing countries." "Oil bureaucracy and development" was the topic of the second meeting, which was held in Bahrain. A preparatory committee held the first special meeting and the first general meeting in Bahrain in December 1980 and decided, based on the views of those present, to establish the development panel (*Nadwat al-Tanmiya*). The founding members included 26 people[2] (Appendix C). Some of the most productive scholars of the group are Dr. Usama Abd al-Rahman of Saudi Arabia, Dr. Ali Khalifa al-Kuwari of Qatar, Dr. Ali Musi of Kuwait, Dr. Muhammad al-Rumaihi of Kuwait, and Dr. Hasan Abdalla Fakhro of Bahrain.

The general objective of *Nadwat al-Tanmiya* is "to create an intellectual and scientific environment which would promote contact and exchange of views in this region among those interested in development issues and which would spend the effort to study the conditions of development, examine its constraints and explore solutions."[3]

In order to achieve this general objective *Nadwat al-Tanmiya* strives to do several specific tasks:[4] To strengthen contacts among those interested in the development of the region; to identify the unique nature of development in the region, rather than emulate other development experiments in other societies; to arouse the desire and incentive in the region to tackle environmental issues and relate them to general questions of development; to expand awareness regarding the application of practical systems and the management of development, which would allow the region to best utilize its resources; and to exchange expertise and knowledge, to benefit from successful experiments, and to avoid duplication of efforts.

In order to attain its goals, *Nadwat al-Tanmiya* has conducted a series of activities:[5]

(1) an annual meeting for the exchange of views about a major topic that is strategically linked to the process of development. This exchange of views could focus on either one principal study or a review of other studies and experiments; (2) supervising specialized studies that have a direct and significant impact on the future of development in the region; one of the members would be charged with preparing the study and moderating the discussion of the study at the meeting; (3) holding meetings, panels, and conferences according to the decision of the preparatory committee.

The meetings are attended by the members and by others who are invited by the preparatory committee.

Initially, *Nadwat al-Tanmiya* was to be administered by a preparatory committee, whose members are selected by the standing committee, and by a coordinator. It was to be financed from the following sources:[6] Membership dues, a minimum of 200 Kuwaiti dinars annually; contributions by members; income from panels, conferences, and studies; contributions from foundations and individuals, as long as these contributions do not contradict the objectives of the *Nadwat al-Tanmiya*; interest that might accrue from investment of the *Nadwat al-Tanmiya*'s capital.

As of January 1985, *Nadwat al-Tanmiya* had 40 members including professors, administrators, writers, publishers, businessmen, ministers, and bankers. The membership is drawn from Kuwait (14), Saudi Arabia (9), Qatar (7), Bahrain (5), United Arab Emirates (3), and Iraq (1). Iraq is not a member of the GCC. Table 4.1 gives a breakdown of the membership by profession.

Table 4.1 *Nadwat al-Tanmiya*: Breakdown of Membership by Profession (as of January 1985)

Profession	Number
Corporate directors	9
University administrators	4
Editors/writers/publishers	3
Bankers	2
Businessmen	7
Ministers/deputy ministers	2
Teachers/professors	5
Other government officials	4
Directors of regional organizations	3
Judges	1
Total	40

Source: Compiled by the author.

Between 1979 and 1985, *Nadwat al-Tanmiya* held six annual meetings to discuss special studies prepared for those meetings. These development-related studies are usually written by a member of the group at the request of the executive committee. A draft of the study is distributed to the members prior to the meeting. Following the annual meeting, the author rewrites the study, taking into consideration the views and suggestions voiced at the meeting. Table 4.2 lists the studies and their authors.

In this chapter, the annual *Nadwat al-Tanmiya* studies will be examined in detail. However, a few introductory remarks are in order. First, the reader will notice much overlapping in some of the topics discussed. For example, manpower planning is treated in the studies on bureaucracy, education, population, and publicly owned projects. In a sense, the duplication might be useful because of the fact that these topics are treated from different perspectives. Second, although critical of the status quo, these studies have offered some rational solutions to the serious problems that they see hindering the process of development. Third, the authors of these studies have based their studies on a common definition of development. This definition, which is the underpinning of *Nadwat al-Tanmiya*'s entire approach to future development in the oil-producing states of the Gulf, is as follows:

Table 4.2 *Nadwat al-Tanmiya*: List of Studies, Authors, and Places and Dates of Annual Meetings

No.	Place of Meeting	Date of Meeting	Title of Study	Author
1	Abu Dhabi	December 1979	Role of Public Projects in Economic Development in the Oil-Producing States of the Arabian Peninsula[a]	Ali Khalifa
2	Bahrain	December 1980	Oil Bureaucracy and the Problem of Development[b]	Usama Abd al-Rahman
3	Not Available		Indigenous Labor Force and Its Significance for Self-Reliance	Sulayman Abd al-Razzaq al-Mutawwa'
4	Kuwait	January 1983	Role of Industry in the Oil-Producing States of the Arabian Peninsula	Industrial Consulting Office, Kuwait
5	Abu Dhabi	January 1984	Education and Development	Abd al-Aziz al-Jalal
6	Bahrain	January 1985	Population Policy and the Future of Development	Ali al-Musa

[a]Published as a book in 1983
[b]Published as a book in 1982
Source: Compiled by the author.

> Comprehensive development is a conscious societal process which aims at creating a certain transformation in the socio-economic structure that through self-reliance would result in a steady increase in the per capita real income for the foreseeable future. This transformation would also create a new socio-political relationship which would guarantee basic individual political freedoms and rights through which the individual's long-term security and stability would be enhanced.[7]

The authors also agreed on a common definition of two other terms: "public administration" and "a publicly owned project." "Public administration" is defined as "a structure encompassing all ministries, bureaus, and centralized agencies whose budgets are part of the general budget of the state, and which are not administered independently—either legally or financially."[8] A "publicly owned project" is "defined as a legally independent entity that is wholly or partially owned and directly operated by the public sector for the purpose of profit making."[9] The remainder of this chapter will consist of an examination of the annual studies of *Nadwat al-Tanmiya*. A chronological approach will be taken.[10]

PUBLICLY OWNED PROJECTS AND DEVELOPMENT

This topic was the subject of the first annual meeting of *Nadwat al-Tanmiya*. The study was based on field research via a questionnaire sent to 51 officials of publicly owned projects and on at least 60 interviews conducted by the author of the study over a two-year period.

This study, together with the other five annual studies, has focused on three basic terms: "comprehensive socio-economic development," "public administration," and "public projects." In addition, the study examined the social, political, and environmental factors affecting comprehensive development. Among these factors are education, manpower planning, bureaucracy, and population policy. Hence, it becomes apparent that the issues examined in this series of studies are organically linked to the policies, plans and objectives of the GCC.

During the discussion of the draft study in December 1979, the audience raised two central questions: (1) What is the nature of public projects in the oil producing states of the Gulf? (2) What is the role which public projects should play in the process of economic development in the region?[11]

They also raised several other related questions, including the following: To what extent is public ownership of projects compatible with the nature of present economic and political systems? What are the societal returns from publicly owned projects? How should the present generation invest the oil revenues (which are obtained from publicly owned projects) in order to secure a decent life for future generations? Should these revenues be invested, deposited in savings institutions, or given out as loans? How can the state supervise publicly owned projects, particularly when the state must perform two separate functions: a protector of the public interest and an economic investor? Is it possible to separate these two functions? Can some of these publicly owned projects be administered as legally independent entities, or should they be managed by government ministries and agencies? How are the administrators (officers and boards of directors) of publicly owned projects chosen? Are existing laws and procedures sufficient? To what extent do Gulf public projects apply modern public administration methods?[12]

Several conclusions emerged from the discussion of the draft study:

1. For publicly owned projects to play a significant role in economic development, the purpose for their existence must be clearly defined.
2. An indigenous cadre of trained career managers must be developed to run these publicly owned projects.
3. The Gulf states themselves must encourage the management of these projects to function effectively. For these projects to perform successfully in the development of the region, they must be based on sound public administration principles. These principles involve setting of goals and objectives, decision making, policy planning, appointment and promotion of officers, financial planning, and use of available human and material resources.[13]
4. Public projects must be separated—administratively, legally, and functionally—from government departments. Although these projects must ultimately be responsible to a specific ministry, they should have their own appointed boards of directors.[14]
5. Job descriptions of the officers of these projects must be clearly delineated, and an effective supervision system must be established to evaluate the performance of project officers. At the same time, they should allow a reasonable degree of administrative autonomy.
6. An environment must be created that is conducive to functioning effectively. Unfortunately, constraints exist in the form of early promotions, excessive consumption of consumer goods due to abundance, the international nature of the oil business, and the absence of an indigenous pool of trained managers.[15]

BUREAUCRACY AND DEVELOPMENT

The second annual study of *Nadwat al-Tanmiya*, entitled *al-Biruqratiyya al-Naftiyya wa Mu'dilat al-Tanmiya* (Oil Bureaucracy and the Problem of Development), was examined by *Nadwat al-Tanmiya* at the second annual meeting in December 1980 in Bahrain.[16]

The objective of this study was to discover the basis of development in the oil-producing countries of the Arabian Peninsula and to examine the factors that contribute to or hinder development. In conducting the study, the author made two assumptions: As a concept, political independence is meaningful only in the context of development. Bureaucracies in the oil countries are a heavy burden that no longer suits the development process; they were set up in another era for other objectives.[17]

The pessimism that characterizes the study regarding the future of comprehensive development in the oil countries is attributed to four factors:

First, the present economic structure, which is dependent on one source (oil), is subject to collapse because the oil will ultimately dry up.

Second, the region is coveted by and subjected to foreign interests and pressures.

Third, there is no serious effort to break the cycle of economic dependency and underdevelopment.

Fourth, there have been many wrong assumptions and poor achievements in the field of development.[18]

Comprehensive development can be achieved through the simultaneous interaction of several elements: a strong economic force; an organized and aware political force; a strong participatory social force; and a competent administrative force.[19] The management of the development process must have the ability to shape policy and define goals; initiate and innovate; face major situations; effect change; change administratively; make informed and objective decisions; and implement decisions competently and effectively.[20]

In fact, the management of the development process in these states lacks the ability to do most if not all of the above. Furthermore, to achieve a truly comprehensive development program, several supports must be present: the will to develop; clearly defined goals and policies; a politically aware leadership; a competent administration; a qualified and adequately trained workforce; a genuine political support; true social interaction; and a productive economic base.[21]

Again, the author argues, these supports do not seem to exist in the oil-producing states of the Arabian Peninsula. Furthermore, development in the oil states seems to involve the importing of the superficialities of civilization from the developed countries—tall buildings, big cars, and technological luxuries for amusement.[22] It also seems that policymakers in the Gulf states are primarily concerned with the economic aspects of development; the social and administrative aspects of development occupy a much lower level in their thinking. Political development is nonexistent. What some see happening in the Gulf is not development but growth.[23]

Effective planning is almost completely lacking in the oil-producing countries, even in those countries that profess to have development plans. Gulf states lack a clear social and economic vision that can be translated into specific goals and objectives. These states must accept the efficacy of comprehensive planning in all of its aspects—economic, administrative, political, and social. Also, they must coordinate their planning efforts. Coordination in this area is the first step to break the cycle of economic dependency. Of course, according to the author, coordination in and of itself does not guarantee elimination of economic dependency. Indeed, many examples of coordination existed in the Gulf prior to the establishment of the GCC yet economic dependency continued to prevail.[24]

The GCC might play a better role in the achievement of regional coordination in development if the question of development is given top priority. First and foremost, a regional development plan must be established for the six GCC states. Second, in the context of this plan, a regional, comprehensive population policy must be adopted, to be followed by regional education and training manpower plans. Basically, comprehensive planning in the GCC should include the following areas: oil production; investment of oil revenues; industrialization; education; training; and manpower.[25]

Bureaucracy in the Gulf states has expanded tremendously. Two factors have contributed to this growth: the lack of a future plan, and the abundance of oil revenues. Gulf bureaucracies suffer from certain disabilities, both structural and behavioral. Gulf bureaucracies remain tribal in nature. That is, they attempt to solve current problems using a tribal or "bedouin" approach.[26]

Bureaucracies in the Gulf states expanded rapidly in the late 1960s and early 1970s without any specific plans and without any real administrative reform. In addition, bureaucracies in GCC states contain a relatively high percentage of uneducated or poorly educated government employees—both indigenous and expatriate. In terms of higher education, a large percentage of university degree holders in the bureaucracy are expatriates. Table 4.3 gives a breakdown of government employees in Qatar.

Abd al-Rahman maintains that administrative reform in government bureaucracies in GCC countries has been disappointing. He cites several reasons: the inability of foreign experts to understand the practical realities in these countries; the tendency to emulate models based on the developed countries; the inability of responsible government agencies to introduce reform; the bureaucratic opposition to

Table 4.3 Government Employees in Qatar According to Educational Level and Citizenship (1980)

	Qatari		Arab		Foreign		Undetermined		Total	
Educational Level	Number	% of Total	Number	% of Total	Number	% of Total	Number	% of Total	Number	% of Total
No qualifications	6,648	32	1,785	8	12,456	60	21	0	20,910	100
Elementary school	751	45	190	11	716	43	–	–	1,657	100
Middle school	909	44	291	14	886	42	–	–	2,086	100
High school	1,438	26	1,443	26	2,648	48	1	0	5,530	100
High school diploma	538	18	1,123	37	1,354	45	–	–	3,015	100
Bachelor's	836	21	2,399	60	783	19	–	–	4,018	100
Advanced diploma	45	7	399	67	156	26	–	–	600	100
Master's	18	6	143	51	118	42	1	0	280	100
Doctorate	10	5	187	89	12	6	–	–	209	100
Other	13	16	6	7	60	75	1	1	80	100
Totals	11,206	29	7,966	21	19,189	50	24	0	38,385	100

Source: Usama Abd al-Rahman, *al Biruqratiyya al-Naftiyya wa Mu'dilat al-Tanmiya* [Oil Bureaucracy and the Problem of Development] (Kuwait: National Council for Culture and the Arts, 1982), p. 117.

administrative reform; administrative reform programs lack political support; a weak feeling of institutional belonging on the part of government employees; the social educational environment; and bureaucratic corruption.[27]

Two supports undergird genuine administrative reform: political and social. Political support involves the adoption of a political program expressing the practical commitment of the country's political leadership to reform as a national interest, not just a mere political slogan. Social support dictates that a comprehensive reform program be adopted in education which would help treat the basic symptoms of administrative problems. An effective cultural program for reform must depend on both education and information.[28]

Education and manpower training are the cornerstone of development in the Gulf states. The small population, the lack of trained manpower, and the heavy expenditures on programs and projects have created a serious problem in development that can be solved only by massive programs for the training of indigenous manpower. These programs would include campaigns to wipe out illiteracy and expansion of formal education and vocational centers.[29]

Education, in particular, suffers from several weaknesses: quantitative expansion without any interest in qualitative improvement; increasing educational costs and decreasing productivity; no coordination between the content of education and the different kinds of educational programs; short-term educational planning and weak educational administrations; and a preponderance of theorizing in education as compared to practical needs.[30]

Universities in the Gulf states suffer from the same problems that other public institutions suffer from: too much government control and a lack of clear objectives as to their role in society. A solution of the university crisis rests on the following: the establishment of a framework for clearly defined goals and expectations that can be realistically attained; the adoption of objective criteria for the selection of university administrations, not influenced by political and social subjective considerations; a guarantee of academic freedom and a suitable environment for scholarly research; a radical change in the philosophy and content of education so that a strong bond can be established between the university and society as a whole. Unfortunately, the universities in the Gulf states are factories for degrees, rather than centers for learning and critical thinking.[31]

In concluding the study, five courses of action are suggested for genuine, comprehensive development: (1) an interest in the individual;

(2) the establishment of clear goals for development based on the general belief that the individual is the center of this process—economically, socially, culturally, and politically; (3) a review of the goals, syllabi, and institutions of education and training; (4) a modernization of the system of civil service to avoid duplication and contradictions; and (5) comprehensive manpower planning.[32]

INDUSTRY AND DEVELOPMENT

In the oil-producing states, industrialization, particularly in petrochemicals, has come to play an important role in the national economy since the late 1970s. The contribution of industry to the national economy of the Gulf countries was the subject of the fourth annual meeting of *Nadwat al-Tanmiya* in January 1983 in Kuwait. The study, entitled "Role of Industry in Building a Productive Base in the Oil Producing States of the Arabian Peninsula," was prepared by the Kuwaiti Industrial Consulting Office.[33]

The study is based on a questionnaire distributed to a selected sample of businessmen and industrialists in Kuwait, Saudi Arabia, Qatar, and Bahrain. The purpose of the study was to solicit their opinion regarding industrial development in these countries. The study focused on the following topics: industrial goals; industrial institutions; negative activities of industry; government support of industry—nature, size and justification; industrial impediments; industrial characteristics and proposed strategies; and Gulf-wide coordination in the area of industrial development.[34]

The industrialists and businessmen who were polled identified four industrial goals: diversification of resources (30.27 percent); a good return on investment (27.85 percent); developing human resources (23.11 percent); and raising the standard of living (18.77 percent).[35] In addition, over half of those interviewed (52.07 percent) felt that the industrial sector can attain these goals, at least partially, even though basic prerequisites such as raw materials and indigenous labor are lacking. Fully 33.35 percent even felt that industrial goals can be completely attained.[36]

Over 70 percent felt that the responsibility of industrializing the country should be assigned to a government ministry (41.2 percent cited the Ministry of Industry and 29.2 percent cited the Ministry of Planning). However, 46.4 percent of those interviewed felt that no coordination exists among these government ministries which would benefit the country. Only 53.6 percent felt that such coordination exists.[37] According to those interviewed, the reasons contributing to this lack of coordination included the following: the absence of a clear industrial policy (21.69 percent); duplication (17.7 percent); the absence of a central executive agency for follow-up purposes (17.57 percent); vagueness of the responsibilities of organizational and executive officers (14.87 percent); weakness of executive agencies due to a lack of expertise (12.75 percent); a multiplicity of agencies and a confusion of organizational goals (9.17 percent); conflict (3.5 percent); and the state economic system (3.75 percent).[38]

The top five reasons are, of course, very serious, and if they are not alleviated, industrial development will always be haphazard. When asked whether government agencies and ministries, which are responsible for industrial planning, perform their responsibilities adequately, those interviewed split in half. Again, when asked to identify the reasons for this poor performance, the interviewees cited similar reasons to those stated above.[39]

Based on their experience in industry, those interviewed were asked to identify the sector that should be put in charge of industrial development. One third identified the private sector; 21.7 percent identified the public sector. However, 44.8 percent felt that industrial development should be the responsibility of both sectors. Those who supported the role of the private sector cited that sector's flexibility. Those who identified the public sector felt that government financial support for industrial projects was crucial.[40]

Domestic industrial expansion has been affected by many negative factors. They include the influx of expatriate labor (26.8 percent); the limited numbers of indigenous labor in the industrial sector (16.2 percent); burdening the national budget with long-term expenses due to government financial support (16.2 percent); rising interest rates on deposits, which led many to invest their money in banks rather than in industry (13.9 percent); and industrial pollution of the environment (11.5 percent).[41] A vast majority of those interviewed felt that industrial expansion resulted in a massive influx of expatriate labor.

When asked to propose ways to encourage indigenous labor to join the industrial sectors, those interviewed identified five ways:

1. to link the educational curricula to the country's needs of industrial labor (28.6 percent);
2. to modernize the methods of current training programs (20.35 percent);
3. to increase the number of educational missions overseas for industrial education (19.3 percent);

4. to revise present legislation concerning industrialization and to require indigenous labor, upon the completion of training, to work in local industries for a specific period of time (17.3 percent); and

5. to have the state give financial support to industrial projects for the purpose of providing indigenous labor with pay raises and financial incentives (14.45 percent).[42]

An overwhelming majority of those interviewed felt that present vocational training centers are incapable of training sufficient indigenous labor force to fill all the jobs in the industrial sector. Again, reasons for this failure were many, including the general educational plan, the failure of the country's public relations agencies to highlight the significance of industrial training; and a lack of corporate interest in training programs. Over 90 percent of those interviewed felt that the establishment of central agencies for vocational training would enhance the process of training for the indigenous labor force.[43]

Responding to a question about the industries that best suit the environment in Gulf countries, the interviewees put petrochemicals at the top of the list (23.95 percent) and textiles at the bottom (5.65 percent). Other industries listed were construction (21.03 percent), foodstuffs (16.15 percent), sewage treatment (15.67 percent), engineering and minerals (10.37 percent), and consumer goods and luxuries (7.17 percent).[44] The respondents also felt that industrial planning in the Gulf countries should be directed toward capital-intensive (as opposed to labor-intensive) industries and should focus on export industries.

On the question of regional industrial coordination, 93.75 percent of those interviewed felt that it did not exist. Yet, they supported this type of coordination.[45]

EDUCATION AND DEVELOPMENT

Education is, of course, at the heart of national policy regarding development. In this context, education involves three primary aspects: national educational policy, school curricula (including vocational and manpower training), and the training and performance of teachers. Three studies were prepared on education and development for the fifth annual meeting of *Nadwat al-Tanmiya*, held in Abu Dhabi in January 1984. These studies focused on the role of education in development, the problems of the educational system, and the training and qualifications of teachers in the Arab world, including an assessment of the teaching profession itself. An examination of the three studies follows.

Education plays a crucial role in the Gulf countries particularly because of the small population, the influx of expatriate labor, the lack of natural resources, other than oil, and the relatively new educational system. Accordingly, the building of educational systems in these countries must be homocentric—that is, the individual must be the focal point. This should be the primary goal of educational development in the Gulf.[46]

Within this goal, five specific objectives must be realized: providing a minimum level of education for all; nurturing intellectual independence and developing creative abilities; strengthening values and productive tendencies; linking secondary and university education to development requirements and the labor market; and developing scientific research and establishing a technological base.[47]

The process of development, according to the author of the study, requires a broad base of educated people. Massive efforts should be spent on expanding education, eliminating illiteracy, encouraging females to get more education, and preparing competent and committed teachers. Current debate in education reveals that the educational system in Gulf states emphasizes surrender, obedience, and acceptance of other views without being convinced of their accuracy. It also encourages people not to speak up even if errors are being committed.[48]

Education must also encourage productivity and the values of physical labor. However, there still exist in Gulf societies negative attitudes, based on tribal and clan status, which denigrate manual labor. Treatment of people is also affected by their social status and tribal origins. All Gulf societies suffer from these attitudes to some degree, a situation that will not change without a complete social and economic reform.[49]

A revision of the educational curricula, particularly in higher education, must be a top priority. Such a revision must aim at making the university responsive to the needs of development through preparing generations of productive, competent, and capable people. Second, Gulf states must revise their whole attitude toward college degrees and college graduates. Presently, Gulf states guarantee their college graduates a job in government regardless of qualifications, which has resulted in inflated national budgets, with per capita expenditures that far exceed those of the United States. In addition, "luxury" unemployment has spread.[50]

New curricula must tighten course requirements as well as admission requirements to universities. Professors must be expected to keep up with their disciplines, and students must be advised to go into the sciences, technological fields, and other professional areas. Gulf countries have an abundance of liberal arts colleges that offer numerous programs in Arabic language and literature, Islamic law, and traditional education programs.[51] This point is illustrated in Table 4.4 which gives a breakdown of students in higher education in the Gulf states in 1980/81.

The author attributes most of the educational problems in the Arab world, and in the Gulf states in particular, to the educational system itself. The second part of his study for the fifth annual meeting of *Nadwat al-Tanimya* addresses this issue.[52]

The study was based on field research and numerous interviews with officials and educational experts. The interviews indicated that a gap exists between awareness of the problems of education and action to reform the system. Most officials agreed that the policymakers in the political system must lead the reform movement and supervise the implementation of reform. That no meaningful reform has

Table 4.4 Student Enrollment in Higher Education in the Gulf According to Country and Field of Specialization (1980/81)

Field	United Arab Emirates	Bahrain	Kuwait	Saudi Arabia	Qatar	Total
Literature	760	187	3,611[a]	15,037	354	19,949
Sciences	445	90	1,623	3,157	265	5,580
Education	461	–	–	7,414	1,005	8,880
Administrative sciences	542	–	2,025	7,765	–	10,332
Shari'a and law	257	–	622	7,884[b]	101	8,864
Agriculture	22	–	–	1,139	–	1,161
Engineering	32	–	993	4,672	45	5,742
Medicine	–	–	429	2,088	–	2,517
Totals	2,519	277	9,312	49,154	1,770	63,025

[a]Includes educational literature.
[b]Includes Islamic studies.

Source: Abd al-Aziz al-Jalal, "Problems of the Educational System and Development" [Arabic] (Abu Dhabi, January 1984), p. 18. Unpublished.

been implemented in the Gulf states may be because these states possess small populations. A second reason might be that they do not have the support of officials in those states.[53] The research indicated that problems in education may be divided into two categories: internal (within the educational system itself) and external (involving the relationship of the educational system to other social systems in society). The internal problems focus on the administration, the teacher, and the curriculum.[54]

Based on the interviews, at least eight major problems were identified in educational administrations: (1) weak administrative ability among school principals and assistant principals; (2) failure to provide a comfortable school environment that would allow for student participation; (3) authoritarian tendencies; (4) school administrators heavily influenced by government bureaucracies in other areas; (5) strong centralization in finance and in policy making even on the local school level; (6) decisions frequently made without adequate studies of the potential results of such decisions; (7) school buildings that are poor, overcrowded, and unsuitable for education; (8) a gap between declared goals and policies and the actual implementation of policy.[55]

When asked to identify some of the major problems pertaining to the teacher, interviewed officials identified five: small number of indigenous teachers; lack of expertise among indigenous teachers and a poor commitment to the teaching profession; absence of a democratic atmosphere which would allow for teacher participation thereby resulting in teacher apathy and low morale; low esteem of teachers in the eyes of the society as a whole; and teacher moonlighting for additional income.[56]

The study also revealed even more dissatisfaction with the school curriculum. Indeed, those interviewed identified at least eleven problems: (1) repetition and duplication of information from year to year; (2) poorly defined objectives; (3) too much material, which forces the student to memorize rather than absorb the content intellectually; (4) the curriculum unrelated to the modern age; (5) outdated information, which often relies on translations from, and copying of, other sources; (6) no attention paid to special students—either the gifted and talented or those with a learning disability; (7) weak English-language curriculum; (8) religious education occupying too large a portion of the curriculum, which is taught through memorization; (9) students taught to obey authority and discouraged from showing initiative and creativity; class participation and discussion not tolerated; (10) political socialization and citizenship are weak components of the curriculum; and (11) predominance of the liberal arts over the sciences in the curriculum.[57]

When asked to offer solutions to the above problems, those interviewed recommended that the educational system should attempt to attain certain specific objectives:

To create an Arab individual capable of giving and receiving criticism and of handling problems.

To nurture love and respect for work and self-reliance and to encourage initiative, creativity, and a positive attitude toward labor and vocational training.

To reduce the general offerings in the curriculum and to concentrate instead on Arabic and English languages and on the sciences and technological fields.

To strengthen citizenship education and the feeling of national belonging.

To develop an aptitude for thinking, meditation, and reflection rather than rote memory and regurgitation.

To recertify teachers through competency tests.

To democratize the school administration.

To encourage students to pursue self-education.

To provide an atmosphere of academic freedom that would allow for independent scholarly research and exchange of ideas without fear of retribution.

To encourage women to go into teaching, at least on the elementary level, in order to solve the manpower problem.

To encourage teachers to keep up with the research in their fields and to specialize in elementary education.[58]

In the part of the study dealing with the teacher in the Arab world, Dr. Abd al-Aziz al-Jalal made some very interesting observations.[59] He said that the picture of the teacher in the Arab world, including the Gulf states, is not a pretty one. Most grade school teachers do not possess the necessary qualifications to teach, with a vast majority of them having not more than high school education.[60]

Another fact is that the teaching profession does not attract many people with strong abilities. High school students have cited several reasons for their lack of interest in a teaching career: low salaries, limited opportunity for promotion, limited incentives, and a lack of respect by society.[61]

POPULATION AND DEVELOPMENT

Population policy in the GCC states was the focus of the sixth annual meeting of *Nadwat al-Tanmiya* held in Bahrain in January 1985. The study, which was prepared by a Kuwaiti scholar, revealed that population statistics and population policies vary greatly from one country to the next.[62] The author made six general introductory comments.

First, in the Gulf states, population data are treated as a sensitive topic bordering on being as state secret. Accordingly, population estimates in these states vary, depending on the source. Second, indigenous labor is less than half of the total labor force. Third, the population in Gulf countries increased enormously in the 1970s, primarily due to the influx of expatriate labor. Fourth, the nature of the population and concomitant population policy are directly linked to development. Fifth, there is a serious population problem in the GCC states, quantitatively and qualitatively, which will have a far-reaching effect on all other aspects of those societies, including security and the quality of life in general. Sixth, no serious population policy has been introduced in these states to address this problem.[63]

The study also indicated that the actual contribution of the indigenous population in the productive sectors of the economy is very limited and decreasing. Instead, the indigenous population is concentrating in government bureaucracy while expatriates are playing a bigger role in the economic sphere.[64]

According to Dr. al-Musa, the population problem is multi-dimensional: political, economic, social, security, national, international, and, of course, developmental.[65] Table 4.5 gives a breakdown of the indigenous and expatriate labor force in GCC countries.

A particularly serious problem centers on the absence of women's participation in the developmental process. Women constitute half of the population. Therefore, the talk about increasing citizen participation in the labor force "remains hypocritical and meaningless unless the question of women participation in the labor force is addressed."[66] The fact is that in most Gulf countries, women are discouraged from playing more than a marginal role in the economy, in the body politic, and in society at large. Although female students constitute 30-50 percent of the student body throughout the different levels of education, and although a vast majority of them graduate, once they receive the degree, they do not apply their education to productive careers. The Arab, Islamic, tribal tradition in Gulf countries does not provide

Table 4.5 Indigenous and Expatriate Labor Force Estimates in GCC States (1985)

Country	Total Labor Force	Indigenous Labor Force	Expatriate Labor Force	% of Indigenous To Total
	(in thousands)			
United Arab Emirates	670	95	575	14.2
Bahrain	190	80	110	42.1
Saudi Arabia	3,375	1,975	1,400	58.5
Oman	445	245	200	55.0
Qatar	137	27	110	19.7
Kuwait	585	145	440	24.8
Total	5,402	2,567	2,635	47.5

Source: Ali al-Musa, "Population and the Future of Development in the Oil Producing States of the Arabian Peninsula" [Arabic], prepared for *Nadwat al-Tanmiya* (Bahrain, January 1985), p. 193. Unpublished.

women with the opportunity—socially or culturally—to become productive members of society. Half the population is basically shut out.[6 7]

NOTES

1. Nadwat al-Tanmiya li Duwal al-Jazira al-Arabiyya al-Muntija li al-Naft, "Provisional By-Laws" [Arabic] (Bahrain, 1980). Unpublished. Hereinafter cited as "Provisional By-Laws."
2. Ali Khalifa al-Kuwari, *Role of Publicly Owned Projects in Economic Development* (Beirut: Lebanon: Beirut Establishment for Printing and Binding, 1983), pp. 163-72.
3. "Provisional By-Laws," p. 1.
4. Ibid., pp. 1-2.
5. Ibid., p. 2.
6. Ibid., p. 3.
7. Al-Kuwari, *Role*, p. 11.
8. Ibid., p. 12.
9. Ibid.
10. Since the author was unable to obtain a copy of the third study, it will not be included in this analysis.
11. Al-Kuwari, *Role*, pp. 179-80.
12. Ibid., pp. 182-83.
13. Ibid., pp. 150-1.
14. Ibid., p. 152.
15. Ibid., pp. 157-8.

16. Usama Abd al-Rahman, *Oil Bureaucracy and the Problem of Development* (Kuwait: National Council for Culture and the Arts, 1982).
17. Ibid., pp. 8-9.
18. Ibid., p. 9.
19. Ibid., p. 25.
20. Ibid., pp. 30-31.
21. Ibid., p. 31.
22. Ibid., pp. 31-34.
23. Ibid., pp. 35-44.
24. Ibid., pp. 84-85.
25. Ibid., pp. 86-88.
26. Ibid., p. 106. See also Muhammad al-Rumaihi, *Social and Economic Constraints of Development* (Kuwait: Kazima Publishers, 1977).
27. Ibid., pp. 147-66.
28. Ibid., p. 168.
29. Ibid., pp. 204-05.
30. Ibid., p. 226.
31. Ibid., pp. 238-39.
32. Ibid., pp. 316-20. See also a review of Abd al-Rahman's study in *Journal of the Gulf and the Arabian Peninsula Studies* [Arabic], vol. 11, no. 42 (April 1985), pp. 213-19.
33. "Role of Industry in Building a Productive Base in the Oil-Producing States of the Arabian Peninsula" [Arabic] (Kuwait: Industrial Consulting Office, 1983), unpublished.
34. Ibid., p. 1.
35. Ibid., p. 4.
36. Ibid., p. 7.
37. Ibid., pp. 10-12.
38. Ibid., p. 14.
39. Ibid., pp. 16-18.
40. Ibid., pp. 23-24.
41. Ibid., pp. 26-27.
42. Ibid., p. 32.
43. Ibid., pp. 39-42.
44. Ibid., p. 72.
45. Ibid., p. 79.
46. Abd al-Aziz al-Jalal, "Role of Education in Development" [Arabic] (Abu Dhabi, UAE, 1984), p. 5, unpublished.
47. Ibid., pp. 6-7.
48. Ibid., p. 8.
49. Ibid., p. 9.
50. Ibid., pp. 10-11.
51. Ibid., p. 16.
52. Abd Al-Aziz al-Jalal, "Problems of the Educational System and Development" [Arabic] (Abu Dhabi, UAE, 1984), unpublished.
53. Ibid., pp. 1-2.
54. Ibid., p. 3.
55. Ibid., p. 5.

56. Ibid., p. 6.
57. Ibid., pp. 7-8.
58. Ibid., pp. 11-13.
59. Abd al-Aziz al-Jalal, "The Arab Teacher: Training, Qualifications, and the Teaching Profession" [Arabic] (Abu Dhabi, UAE, 1984), unpublished.
60. Ibid., p. 3.
61. Ibid., p. 6.
62. Ali al-Musa, "Population Policy and the Future of Development in the Oil-Producing States of the Arabian Peninsula" [Arabic] (Bahrain, 1985), unpublished.
63. Ibid., pp. 7-8.
64. Ibid., pp. 21-27.
65. Ibid., pp. 30-35.
66. Ibid., p. 121.
67. Ibid., p. 123.

5
OTHER GULF VIEWS OF THE GCC

In addition to the official and the reformist views of the GCC discussed above (chapters 3 and 4), the Gulf Cooperation Council has been the subject of discussion in three other groups: intellectuals not necessarily members of *Nadwat al-Tanmiya*, public opinion makers, and the print media. The first of these three groups is mainly comprised of academics who have written about the GCC, often critically. Although cautiously optimistic about the future of the organization, they nonetheless point to the multitude of problems that the GCC must overcome if it is to succeed. A sample of their writings is presented below.

Assessing public attitudes toward the GCC was made possible by an opinion survey conducted by two professors in Kuwait in the fall of 1984. This was the first, and so far the only, survey of its kind in the Gulf. While the Kuwaiti public strongly supports the GCC, some very interesting responses were given. The study, which was published in June 1985, will be analyzed below.

Press coverage of the GCC will also be addressed in this chapter. Gulf press is in general heavily influenced by government, ranging from almost total control in Oman to minimal control in Kuwait. Every Gulf country has encouraged significant coverage of the activities of the GCC. Most of the reporting is admittedly based on official press releases; however, a review of news items of the last four years gives the reader a clear picture of the media's role in creating public awareness of the GCC and its activities. As was stated in the introduction to this book, it would not be an exaggeration to say that the GCC has been the premier media event of the past five years.

INTELLECTUALS AND THE GCC

Early in 1981, just prior to the signing of the GCC charter, a series of articles appeared in Kuwait's *al-Qabas* newspaper. The articles consisted of interviews with Kuwaiti intellectuals about the Gulf Cooperation Council.[1] They included Dr. Muhammad al-Rumaihi, professor of sociology; Dr. Muhammad Rashid al-Fil, professor of geography; Dr. Adil al-Tabtaba'i, professor of law; Dr. Walid Mubarak, professor of political science; and Dr. Muhammad Abd al-Ghani Sa'udi, professor of political geography.

In those interviews, the Kuwaiti academics expressed qualified support for the GCC. However, they expressed certain reservations about the future success of this regional cooperative effort. For example, Dr. al-Rumaihi noted that although the GCC was a step forward, internal stability and regional security are organically linked and that internal stability must be primarily based on "social justice and political participation."[2]

Dr. al-Fil argued that food (production and availability) is a principal component of security. He also stated that the shortage of foodstuffs and the lack of sufficient indigenous trained manpower would be a serious threat to regional cooperation.[3] Although most of these intellectuals stressed that it was still too early (1981) to predict the future success of the GCC, they urged that organization's leaders to promote Arab unity; encourage popular participation in government; bridge the gap between the rulers and their peoples; support the Palestinian people; encourage a more equitable distribution of wealth; chart a more neutral course for the Gulf in international relations; and discourage any close military relations with the superpowers that would invite any foreign military presence in the region.[4]

As was indicated in the preceding chapters, Gulf intellectuals have continued to express somewhat critical views about the GCC in the intervening four years. In reviewing recent opinions of these same intellectuals, one notices more emphasis on internal issues–economic, social, and political. One of the most vocal of this group is Dr. Abdalla Fahd al-Nafisi, a political science professor and a member of the Kuwaiti National Assembly. Some of his strongest views on the GCC were expressed in a book published in Arabic in London in 1982.[5] In this book, al-Nafisi viewed the establishment of the GCC as a function of the "interest, policies, and perceptions of the two superpowers."[6]

Commenting on the structure and accomplishments of the GCC, al-Nafisi made several points:

1. Constitutional structures based on written constitutional documents must be established.
2. Democratic forms of governing through direct popular elections must be emphasized.
3. The GCC does not allow for new membership. Question: Is the GCC a regional organization or a military alliance?
4. GCC member states, while professing neutrality in the East-West conflict, are in fact tied closely to the United States.
5. Finally, although there have been many public professions of the desire to cooperate economically, in fact very little economic cooperation among the GCC states has developed.[7]

In focusing on security as a principal function of the GCC, al-Nafisi posed the following question: Is the security problem that GCC states face truly military or is it in fact political? Isn't the security problem in essence internal—reflecting a certain relationship between the rulers and their peoples?[8]

In responding to this question, al-Nafisi argued that internal security is usually maintained by one of three methods: (a) supression, harassment, and denial of freedoms; (b) cooptation; and (c) open and direct dialogue with the people. He maintained that some GCC states follow the first method; others the second; and none the third.[9] Among the principal problems facing the organization, according to al-Nafisi, are the following: economic dependency on the capitalist world; political underdevelopment in terms of state institutions; GCC defense being directly linked to U.S. strategic planning; demography and population; and unsettled border disputes.[10]

In addition, tribalism and religious affiliation are still very divisive forces in society. "They remain the primary points of reference."[11] Al-Nafisi agrees with other Gulf intellectuals on the major causes of the population crisis in the Gulf: small indigenous populations, a limited indigenous labor force, lack of women's participation in the economy, and a low educational level of the population.[12]

Al-Nafisi is not optimistic about the future of real development in the region. He expects more violence and political instability. In his view, the GCC states are not ready for political development, nor are they clear as to what path to follow in this regard. "Political reform in the GCC states has become subject to all kinds of domestic and external pressures."[13] He also maintains that corruption pervades high levels of government.

In concluding his study, al-Nafisi argued that "in its present structure, the GCC is just another way to perpetuate the member states' tribal regimes and their continued dependency on the capitalist world."[14]

In June 1985, Dr. al-Nafisi announced his intention to resign from the Kuwaiti National Assembly and return to academia. In a newspaper interview on the subject, he made several important points:

1. Administrative and bureaucratic reform is necessary, and it cannot occur without a reform of the leadership.

2. Human resources must be protected and utilized correctly. Policymakers must have a clear idea of the nature of the population, and they must identify the gaps that presently exist in the administrative structure of the state.

3. A specific agency must be set up with the responsibility of supervising human resources in the state, and it must synchronize the specializations of college students and the needs of the state. The present situation poses a great danger to Gulf societies, particularly in view of the escalating influx of foreign labor.

4. Bureaucratic routine, complacency, and administrative inefficiency also pose serious dangers to society, because they do not encourage genuine reform. Administrative reform, top to bottom, is the main issue.[15]

In commenting on the recent phenomenon of terrorism in the GCC states, particularly in Kuwait, Dr. al-Nafisi stated in the same interview that he expected terrorism and violence to increase in the coming years. Terrorism in the Gulf is directly influenced by many factors, including the continuing Iraq-Iran war, the economic recession, maldistribution of wealth, and the demographic structure of the population. The numerous violent terrorist acts in the Gulf in recent years—Mecca 1979, Bahrain 1981, Kuwait 1984 and 1985—indicate the link between violence and the factors mentioned above. Dr. al-Nafisi's thesis is that violence is caused by economic conditions; economic crises, bankruptcies, unemployment, and recession breed dissatisfaction, which in turn breeds violence.[16] In the long run, argues al-Nafisi, real security can only be guaranteed by representative government.

In a December 1984 lecture "The Gulf Cooperation Council: Challenges and Responses," Dr. Muhammad al-Rumaihi of Kuwait argued that the GCC was a modern legal expression of traditional ties among Gulf Arab societies, and that these ties go far back in time, even though people now cite 1981 as the year in which these ties were formalized.

Cultural ties among the peoples of the Gulf have existed for centuries; men of letters have roamed the region freely regardless of boundaries.[17]

According to al-Rumaihi, the challenges presently faced by GCC states are of two kinds: external (political and military) and internal (developmental). The original Arab state system of the 1960s could not respond to the unique challenges the Gulf states faced in the early 1970s. The establishment of the GCC in the early 1980s was therefore a practical, rational, and realistic response by Gulf states to these challenges.[18]

In the external sphere, argues al-Rumaihi, GCC states have agreed on several operational points:

1. The GCC agreement protects their common interests.
2. The new regional entity determines its own relations with other regional and international organizations.
3. The new entity has its own economic cultural and military program, which it hopes to apply within member countries.
4. This agreement does not prevent member states from disagreeing on some issues that are not considered fundamental.
5. The defense of the Gulf is the responsibility of its people, to be achieved through the establishment of a common military defense capability.[19]

The thrust of Professor al-Rumaihi's thesis is that the GCC faces its most serious challenge on the domestic front, primarily in the areas of planning and development. Accordingly, he made the following observations: To date, development in the Gulf has emphasized quantity, not quality; a clear concept of comprehensive development is still lacking. A need exists to identify the constraints on development—social, political, cultural, and economic. If the GCC is to play a credible regional role, a suitable cultural and political environment must be devised to allow for creative and rational debate of the issues. Finally, Gulf citizens must play a major role in promoting cooperation among Gulf societies.[20]

Addressing the issue of development from a different perspective, Dr. Hasan Fakhro, a Bahraini intellectual, said in a lecture entitled "Crisis of Oil, Development and Man in the Gulf," that over the years cheap energy, while helping the West develop and industrialize, gave the Arab world very little.[21] The oil-producing countries lost many opportunities in the 1974-83 decade by failing to develop strong economic structures.

Dr. Fakhro argued that these oil countries urgently need to rebuild their economic structures to allow for complementarity rather than competition. Secondly, future economic progress requires the adoption of radical changes in the socio-economic fabric of society. Such changes would include educational planning, manpower training, consumer education, and planning and development policies. A policy that aims at balanced, comprehensive planning must be adopted.[22]

Moving from economic planning and development to the political realm, Dr. Kamal al-Manufi, a political science professor at the University of Kuwait, maintains that the absence of democratic institutions in the entire Arab world will also adversely affect the future prospects of the GCC.[23] In his analysis of the crisis of democracy, Professor al-Manufi offered several very interesting observations.[24]

First, the vast majority of people in Arab society do not feel that they have any influence on the political life in that society. They feel unable to criticize their political leaders openly and candidly. Consequently, political apathy and negativism pervade Arab society, and there is no meaningful political participation.

Second, different political opinions are not tolerated in Arab society, particularly opinions that contradict official policy.

Third, other attributes of democracy, such as political initiative, political confidence, and the supremacy of law do not seem to exist in Arab society today. Also lacking are the traditional institutions of democracy: representative assemblies, parliaments, free political parties, and popular political organizations. In the Gulf, only Kuwait has a representative assembly.

Fourth, the school as an agent of political socialization does not seem to inculcate the concept of participating citizenship. Most textbooks emphasize the role of the state and minimize the role of the individual. Educational institutions on all levels, including universities, do not seem to encourage individual initiative. They tend to perpetuate the role of the state and state control, even over the academic endeavors of the professors.

The role of state control in higher education is best illustrated in a series of confidential letters written in 1982, 1983, and 1984 from the Saudi cabinet to university directors and administrators of higher education. Some Saudi academics have cited these letters as an example of the denial of academic freedom in Saudi society.

In a "secret" message from the deputy prime minister to the minister of higher education in 1982, Saudi and non-Saudi professors at King Saud University were ordered to receive prior approval from the government before serving on any scholarly panels, including the "purely scientific ones." The directive stated that approval of participation must be obtained two months in advance.[25]

In a "secret, urgent, and very important" message to department heads from King Saud University's director for higher education and scholarly research, they were requested not to nominate any member of their staff—administrators or faculty—to participate in any conference, panel, or symposium outside the kingdom "without first informing us of said conference and the intended nomination."[26] Requests not submitted at least two months before the date of the conference would not be reviewed.

A third example cited by Gulf academics as a denial of academic freedom is a "secret" cable sent from the Saudi minister of higher education to the chancelors of all Saudi universities. The cable stated that "it is forbidden for the university to contact any government official for the purpose of giving a lecture or participating in a panel before such a request is communicated to us for permission. . . . This directive must be implemented closely and universally."[27]

Finally, the minister of education was told in a "secret" letter from the Saudi minister of interior that according to Royal Directive No. 2443/8, dated 15/11/1404 H. (1984), scholarly theses and dissertations that deal with any subject pertaining to the Kingdom of Saudi Arabia must be presented upon completion, but before presentation to the university, to a special committee connected with the Saudi Supreme Council for Universities. The function of this government committee is to discuss the contents of these scholarly theses.[28]

PUBLIC OPINION AND THE GCC

The first public opinion survey to measure the public's attitudes toward the GCC was conducted by two professors at the University of Kuwait in the fall of 1984. A summary of the study was published in a Kuwaiti newspaper in November 1984;[29] the full study was published in June 1985.[30] This section of the chapter will address the survey and its findings. The survey attempted to elicit public attitudes on six major questions:

1. To what extent is Kuwaiti public opinion interested in, and knowledgeable about, the GCC and how is this interest affected by age, educational level, profession, marital and social status?
2. What factors are perceived by Kuwaiti public opinion as having led to the establishment of the GCC?

3. To what extent is Kuwaiti public opinion doubtful about real security coordination among GCC states?
4. How does Kuwaiti public opinion view the issue of genuine economic complementarity (*takamul*), the movement of labor, and cultural cooperation among GCC member states?
5. What are the constraints on Gulf cooperation?
6. How does Kuwaiti public opinion relate the GCC experiment to the larger question of comprehensive Arab unity?[31]

A sample of 1,000 respondents was selected at random from Kuwait's four districts. The sample consisted mostly of males (79.9 percent), between the ages of 20 and 40 (64.2 percent), married (58.2 percent), educated (53.1 percent high school and 30.8 percent university), employed by government (42.4 percent), and middle class (62.5 percent).[32]

The survey consisted of 98 questions, distributed as follows:

1. Personal data of respondents (6 questions).
2. Interest in the GCC (11 questions).
3. Reasons for the establishment of the GCC (4 questions).
4. Activities and achievements of the GCC (55 questions).
5. Impediments to cooperation (10 questions).
6. Linkage between Gulf cooperation and general Arab cooperation (12 questions).[33]

Following is a summary of the responses.

Interest in the GCC

Of the respondents 58.3 percent correctly identified the year in which the GCC was established; 37.5 percent did not.

Over 95 percent of all respondents correctly identified the six members of the GCC; over 81 percent indicated, again correctly, that Iraq and the two Yemens were not members of the GCC.

Identified the city where the GCC is headquartered—68.8 percent.

Knew that the secretary-general of the GCC is a Kuwaiti national—85.6 percent.

Indicated that they follow GCC news regularly—77.8 percent.

Indicated that they discuss GCC issues occasionally—66.6 percent; 16.8 percent do that regularly; and 16.6 percent do not discuss GCC issues at all.

In terms of the respondents' interest in the specific issues of the GCC, 75.5 percent identified security and political issues to be of primary concern to them. Another 29.4 percent identified economic issues as the primary concern; 22.4 percent identified social issues as their primary concern.[34]

Reasons for the Establishment of the GCC

Respondents were asked to express their opinion on 16 statements that focus on concepts of security, political coordination, economic cooperation, social, cultural, and political similarities of the GCC states, and democratic orientation. Following is a breakdown of the responses:

Felt that the GCC was established to strengthen relations among the member states in all fields–security, politics, and economics–90.3 percent.

Felt that political similarities among the six states contributed to the establishment of the GCC–78.2 percent.

Felt that the GCC was established to protect the region from the designs of foreign powers–73.4 percent.

Felt that the GCC was established as a response to the Iranian revolution–22.5 percent.

Felt that the GCC was established as a response to the Iraq-Iran war–31.5 percent.

Felt that the GCC was established as a response to the Soviet invasion of Afghanistan–21.9 percent.

Felt that the GCC was established to protect the security of its member states–86.7 percent.

Rejected the statement that the GCC was a creation of the United States–67 percent; 15.5 agreed with the statement.

Felt that the threat of diminishing oil reserves was one reason for establishing the GCC–34.4 percent.

Felt that the desire to achieve economic cooperation among the Gulf states was a factor in establishing the GCC–73.6 percent.

Felt that one of the factors behind the establishment of the GCC was the desire to invest oil revenues in domestic projects–54.8 percent.

Felt that the GCC was established to promote political coordination among the members–82.6 percent.

Felt that societal similarities among the six states contributed to the establishment of the GCC–83.1 percent.

Felt that the GCC was an organization of the ruling families only–26.6 percent; 54.8 percent rejected the statement.

Felt that the GCC opposes democracy–37.3 percent; 39.7 percent rejected the statement.

Felt that the GCC aims at undermining the democratic experiment in Kuwait–24.5 percent.

Felt that the GCC was an organization of both governments and peoples–62.1 percent.

Felt that the GCC expresses the will of the peoples of the region–62.3 percent; 24.5 felt that it did not.

It is interesting to note that a relatively large percentage of "no opinion" was offered in response to sensitive political statements.[35]

Activities and Achievements of the GCC

One of the primary objectives of the GCC, according to official statements, is to ensure that the security and stability of the region are the responsibility of the region's peoples and states. GCC officials have often emphasized the Gulf states' determination to defend their security, independence, and sovereignty. Therefore, it was expected that the respondents in this public opinion poll would overwhelmingly equate the GCC with the security of the region. It should be noted that the respondents seemed to have a more comprehensive view of security than the traditional military one. Following is a summary of their opinions on security-related questions:

Agreed with the statement that the security of the Gulf is the responsibility of the states of the region–not outsiders–84.6 percent.

Rejected the statement that the region's security can be achieved only through the intervention of superpowers–81.2 percent.

Rejected the statement that the region's security can be achieved through coordination with the West, particularly the United States–72 percent.

Felt that the region's security can be achieved by avoiding superpower alliances–80.4 percent.

Felt that building a strong Gulf army is a primary component of regional security–92.3 percent.

Felt that continued military coordination is another primary component of regional security–86.6 percent.

Felt that internal security is linked to democracy–85.5 percent.

Felt that security is linked to social justice–88.4 percent.

Felt that abolishing the Asian labor force in Gulf countries would enhance the region's security–52.7 percent; 30 percent disagreed with this position.

Felt that security coordination among GCC states is possible–68.9 percent.[36]

An analysis of the security question leads to several comments. First, differences of opinion exist among GCC states regarding the concept of security. For example, Kuwait rejects any foreign presence regardless of source and sees the necessity of establishing relations with both East and West. Oman believes that cooperation with the West, especially the United States, will enhance Gulf security.

Second, a difference of opinion also exists regarding democracy and its institutions (for example, a constitution, national assembly, and free press). Again, Kuwait is far ahead of the other states.

Third, Kuwaitis–government and people–have rejected the proposed draft security agreement that has been circulated among GCC members.

As one of the major activities of the GCC, economic cooperation has been pursued, at least according to official statements, through long-range planning regarding the investment of oil revenues, a diversification of the sources of income, building a productive base, and nurturing an indigenous labor force. The desire for economic cooperation and the building of a viable regional economy have led the GCC in 1981 to ratify the ambitious Unified Economic Agreement. Underlying this agreement is the belief that economic complementarity is the key to future progress.

With its questions on the Unified Economic Agreement, general economic cooperation, and the factors which might hinder such cooperation, the survey provoked some interesting reactions.

Supported the Unified Economic Agreement, particularly the establishment of a uniform tariff rate–68.8 percent. However, 40.6 percent felt that the Unified Economic Agreement remains "ink on paper."

Felt that economic cooperation could benefit the peoples of the member states–53.3 percent. However, 37.9 percent felt that economic cooperation would benefit only a small minority of merchants and realtors.

Felt that economic cooperation would be difficult in the shadow of dependency on the capitalist system–58 percent. However, 64.8 percent felt that economic cooperation among GCC states is possible because the basic ingredients for such cooperation are present: raw materials, similar climatic and geological conditions, availability of capital, similar social systems, and geographic proximity.

Supported the establishment of joint economic projects–88.7 percent.

Supported the unifying of tariffs and financial systems–79 percent.

Preferred the investment of oil revenues in projects within the GCC countries rather than depositing them in foreign banks–88.5 percent. This preference was even emphasized in cases where foreign investment might bring more lucrative financial returns than domestic projects.[37]

A major aspect of economic cooperation is expected to focus on the ability of GCC citizens to move, work, and reside freely throughout the six GCC countries. Of the respondents 82 percent supported the free movement, work, and residency of GCC citizens throughout the GCC countries; 45 percent supported extending the right to non-GCC citizens. Seventy-five percent supported the adoption of uniform GCC policies regarding the importation of foreign labor.[38]

Impediments to Cooperation

Since most observers of the GCC agree that real economic cooperation among GCC states faces many impediments, the respondents were asked to express their opinion on several statements identifying some of the potential hindrances. Following is a summary of the responses.

Seventy-one percent rejected the statement that "since economic cooperation already exists among Gulf states, the establishment of the GCC was not necessary." In gauging the impact of the GCC on the level of actual economic cooperation, 42 percent felt that the level of cooperation has increased, 24 percent felt that the level of cooperation has decreased, and 24 percent felt that the level of cooperation has stayed the same.[39]

Forty percent felt that the GCC faces many problems. Among these problems, the respondents identified the following: the absence of elected national assemblies and free press (other than Kuwait), differences in the foreign policies of member states, border disputes, the Gulf war, foreign intervention, lack of a well-trained indigenous labor force, the tendency of Saudi Arabia to dominate the GCC, and the nature of GCC membership. For example, on this last point, 55 percent supported the admission of Iraq and 59 percent supported the admission of North Yemen. It is interesting to note that when asked to identify potential problems, 37 percent expressed no opinion.[40] Table 5.1 gives a breakdown of the responses.

Table 5.1 Respondents' Perception of Hindrances Facing the GCC (percent)

No.	Statement	Agree	Do Not Agree	No Opinion
1.	Border disputes as a hindrance	31.4	41.9	26.7
2.	The GCC General Secretariat is responsive to citizens's complaints	41.6	26.5	31.9
3.	The United States plays a major role in charting and directing the policies of the GCC	27.9	50.2	21.9
4.	Superpower interests in the region is a hindrance	56.9	24.8	18.3
5.	Gulf citizens cannot criticize the GCC because of the lack of political freedom	44.6	34.5	20.9
6.	Disputes among Gulf ruling families is a hindrance	31.4	41.9	26.7
7.	Low political awareness among Gulf peoples is a hindrance	58.7	28.8	12.5

Source: Shamlan Yusif al-Isa and Kamal al-Manufi, *Trends in Kuwaiti Public Opinion Regarding the Gulf Cooperation Council* [Arabic] (Kuwait: University of Kuwait, Department of Political Sciences, 1985), p. 38.

Gulf Cooperation and General Arab Cooperation

In defining the relationship between the GCC and the Arab world, Gulf leaders have made three major points over the years:

1. Coordination and cooperation among Gulf states serve the general goals of the Arab nation.
2. The basic agreement establishing the GCC is in accordance with the Charter of the League of Arab States.
3. The GCC is not an alliance or an axis of states directed against anyone. Rather, it is a coalition of states within the general Arab state system. The survey included several statements on the relationship between the GCC and the Arab world as a whole. Following is a summary of the responses.

Felt that the GCC will have a positive impact on the Arab League–63.1 percent. However, 23 percent did not perceive any impact at all.

Felt that the GCC will strengthen Arab coordination–68.1 percent.

Felt that the GCC will not harm the Arab cause–67.8 percent.

Felt that Gulf security cannot be achieved in the long-term without cooperation and coordination with the rest of the Arab world—59.9 percent.

Felt that Arab security is one indivisible whole—69.8 percent.

Felt that Gulf economic development cannot occur apart from the rest of the Arab world—57.3 percent.

Felt that Arab cooperation is the proper route to follow in order to solve manpower problems in the Gulf states—74.3 percent.

Preferred Arab over Asian labor—83.6 percent.

Preferred Gulf investments in the Arab world over investment in the West, either in Europe or in the United States—91.6 percent.[41]

Concluding Remarks

In reviewing the results of the survey, general conclusions can be drawn:

1. Kuwaiti public opinion reflects a high level of interest in the GCC.
2. Kuwaitis believe that the GCC was established primarily to protect the security of the member states and the region from the ambitions of foreign powers.
3. Kuwaitis strongly support Gulf economic, commercial, industrial, and agricultural coordination. However, they feel that little has been done in this area.
4. Kuwaitis are aware of the many hindrances that impede real cooperative efforts in the Gulf. These constraints are local, regional, and foreign.
5. Kuwaitis are aware of the close linkage between Gulf cooperation and general Arab cooperation.
6. The survey results also revealed the presence of a substantial segment of the Kuwaiti population that has no opinion on GCC matters—either a result of ignorance, or fear, or other reasons. The bulk of this group consists of women, illiterates, single people, and members of the lower class.[42]

Finally, for scholars and students of the contemporary Gulf, this study is valuable for at least three reasons:

1. This is the first public opinion survey in Kuwait or anywhere in the Gulf to measure the people's perceptions of the Gulf Cooperation Council.

2. The results are a quantifiable expression of Kuwaiti thinking about the GCC.

3. This study could become a model for future studies of the whole GCC experiment.[43]

GULF PRESS AND THE GCC

The Gulf Cooperation Council has been covered extensively in the press. Hundreds of articles, news releases, and interviews have been published in regional newspapers and magazines about the GCC. Many of those articles have basically been interviews with GCC officials or reports on speeches given by these officials. Between 1981 and 1985, the press focused more consistently on the GCC than on any other single event or issue in modern times.

This massive press coverage has resulted in two contradictory trends: First, it has expanded the general population's knowledge of the GCC, as revealed in the Kuwaiti public opinion poll; second, it has unwittingly created a gap between the rhetoric and the reality of interstate cooperation. For the most part, press coverage presents a positive and highly optimistic picture of GCC achievements. This is understandable since most of the media are heavily influenced by the respective governments. The perceived gap between rhetoric and reality has largely occurred because the media have failed to emphasize the difficulties encountered in the implementation stage.

For example, since 1982 the Gulf press has strongly supported the ratification of the Unified Economic Agreement. Yet newspaper readers have not been informed of the difficulties of implementing this agreement. Such difficulties are rarely mentioned openly. It was rather unusual that problems in implementing the UEA were even cited by the Omani minister of commerce and industry.[44] Security issues have been treated similarly. For years, the press has rhapsodized about the role of the GCC in protecting Gulf security and about the security treaty that Saudi Arabia has urged for GCC approval. However, Kuwait has consistently refused to ratify the treaty, and the reasons for this refusal have not been explained in the press. In response to this situation, a Gulf official has finally made the lame statement that "GCC states cooperate in security matters with or without written agreements."[45] This sentiment was echoed by Bahrain's prime minister in yet another newspaper interview.[46]

Of course, press coverage of the GCC has been influenced by developments in the region, and since regional security has been of primary concern to Gulf leaders, this issue has dominated the news media. Almost 50 percent of all the newspaper articles since the establishment of the GCC have dealt with regional security. In this context, "security" covers many topics: attempts to destabilize the present regimes, the Iraq-Iran war, Iran's propaganda against the GCC states, the security treaty, arms transfers, terrorism (internal and regional), airplane hijackings, joint military exercises, and the building of strong defenses.[47]

Over 25 percent of all press reports in recent years have dealt with GCC meetings. These meetings can be broken down into three main types: heads of GCC states (Supreme Council); GCC foreign ministers (Ministerial Council); and the GCC secretariat. In recent years, and because of the rise in terrorism, more reporting has been devoted to meetings of GCC interior ministers. However, the annual summits have received the lion's share of press coverage. In addition to newspaper articles, the GCC secretariat itself issues numerous news releases about summits. Furthermore, the host country also contributes many special media reports in anticipation of GCC summits.

A third issue covered in the press has been the GCC's efforts to mediate the Iraq-Iran war. Again, most of the press reports have highlighted GCC efforts to settle the Gulf war, but no serious analysis has been made of its failure to mediate the conflict. The fact is the GCC states, including Saudi Arabia, have been unable to influence either of the two combatants to seek a negotiated settlement. In fact, in a recent newspaper interview, all the Saudi foreign minister would say about the war was that the continuation of the conflict threatened the security of the region.[48]

Gulf newspapers became more vocal on the security question around the middle of 1985 as a reaction to the July terrorist bombings in Kuwait and the assassination attempt on the life of Kuwait's ruler in May of the same year. In response to these terrorist activities, the Gulf press urged GCC leaders to adopt a unified security strategy.[49] In so doing, newspapers were also expressing popular sentiments concerning the events in Kuwait. Furthermore, most editorials stated that the real intention of terrorism in Kuwait was twofold: to undermine the GCC and to threaten the internal stability of its member states.[50]

The foreign ministers devoted their fifteenth meeting as the Ministerial Council of the GCC (July 7-8, 1985, in Abha, Saudi Arabia) to terrorism; the terrorist acts in Kuwait gave the foreign ministers' meeting added significance.[51] Yet press reports have left GCC citizens confused as to the actual accomplishments of the meeting. This confusion has only been heightened by the bomb explosions in Kuwait in late July 1985. To illustrate, let us consider some of the official statements regarding the Ministerial Council's meeting, as reported in the Gulf press:

1. At the conclusion of their meeting in Abha, Saudi Arabia, GCC foreign ministers agreed to take stronger measures against mounting terrorism. Speaking for the group, the Saudi foreign minister, Saud al-Faisal, stated that "recent events in the Gulf require that we increase our cooperation so that we can defend our independence and stability."[52]

2. At their meeting in Abha, Saudi Arabia, GCC foreign ministers placed heavy emphasis on regional security and stability.[53]

3. Most observers agree that the GCC states have embarked on erecting a "Gulf security fence" as a response to the rising wave of terrorism. This possibility was discussed at the GCC Ministerial council meeting in Riyadh on June 24, 1985. Setting up this fence will involve *coordination* among the GCC states, *exchange* of intelligence data, and *cooperation* in security matters.[54]

It is interesting to note that a few weeks prior to the convening of the Ministerial Council, both Kuwaiti and GCC officials spoke out against the joint security treaty that Saudi Arabia has actively pushed within the GCC. On May 22, 1985 it was reported that Kuwait's foreign minister, Shaikh Sabah al-Ahmad al-Jabir, expressed Kuwait's adamant refusal to ratify the joint security treaty.[55] On the eve of the foreign ministers' meeting the GCC secretary-general, Abdallah Bishara, urged Gulf newspapers to "deemphasize the joint security treaty in their coverage."[56] Yet he called for joint security and military efforts on the part of the GCC states and emphasized the concept of self-reliance in defending the region. Said Bishara: "He who sleeps on a foreign arm has nightmares."[57]

In light of the above, it is clear that the Gulf press has played a dual role toward the GCC and toward the public. On the one hand, the press has been a useful source of information about the GCC. On the other hand, the press has created increasingly rising expectations among the peoples of the Gulf regarding the accomplishments of the GCC. Accordingly, the average citizen has little real sense of what the GCC can or cannot do, not only in security but in other areas as well.

NOTES

1. *Al-Qabas*, February 2-28, 1981.
2. *Al-Qabas*, February 7, 1981, p. 5.

3. *Al-Qabas*, February 8, 1981, p. 5.
4. Emile A. Nakhleh, *The Persian Gulf and American Policy* (New York: Praeger, 1982), p. 54.
5. Abdallah Fahd al-Nafisi, *Gulf Cooperation Council: Political and Strategic Context* (London: Ta-Ha Publishers, 1982).
6. Ibid., p. 5.
7. Ibid., pp. 16-17.
8. Ibid., p. 25.
9. Ibid., pp. 26-28.
10. Ibid., p. 32.
11. Ibid., p. 33.
12. Ibid., p. 60.
13. Ibid., p. 50.
14. Ibid., p. 68.
15. *Al-Watan*, June 18, 1985, p. 7.
16. *Al-Qabas*, June 4, 1985, p. 2.
17. *Al-Khaleej* (United Arab Emirates), December 26, 1984, p. 3.
18. Ibid.
19. Ibid.
20. Ibid.
21. *Al-Khaleej* February 26, 27, 28, 1985. The lecture Dr. Fakhro delivered at the Bahrain Reform Society on February 25, 1985 was published in a three-part series in the newspaper.
22. Ibid.
23. Kamal al-Manufi, "Political Culture and the Crisis of Democracy in the Arab World," *al-Watan*, November 11, 1984, p. 6.
24. Ibid.
25. Message No. 7/B/18561, dated 3/8/1402 H. (1982).
26. Message No. 70707/9/T, dated 28/1/1403 H. (1983).
27. Message No. 36/3/5/716/3B, dated 29/2/1404 H. (1984).
28. Message No. 6/5/1576/M, dated 23/11/1404 H. (1984).
29. *Al-Watan*, November 28, 1984, pp. 7-8.
30. Shamlan Yusif al-Isa and Kamal al-Manufi, *Trends in Kuwaiti Public Opinion Regarding the Gulf Cooperation Council* [Arabic] (Kuwait: University of Kuwait, Department of Political Science, 1985).
31. Ibid., pp. 3-4.
32. Ibid., pp. 7-8.
33. Ibid., pp. 9-10.
34. Ibid., pp. 11-12.
35. Ibid., pp. 22-23.
36. Ibid., pp. 24-26.
37. Ibid., pp. 28-30.
38. Ibid., p. 31.
39. Ibid., p. 33.
40. Ibid., pp. 36-37.
41. Ibid., pp. 39-42.
42. Ibid., pp. 101-03.

43. Ibid., p. 104.
44. *Al-Qabas*, July 28, 1985, p. 7.
45. *Al-Watan*, July 11, 1985, p. 1.
46. *Al-Watan*, July 28, 1985, p. 11.
47. *Foreign Broadcast Information Service (FBIS)*, vol. V, June 1, 1981-August 1, 1985. See also the following Gulf newspapers for this period: *al-Qabas* and *al-Watan* of Kuwait, *Akhbar al-Khalij* and *al-Adwa'* of Bahrain, *al-Khaleej* and *al-Bayan* of the United Arab Emirates, and *al-Raya* of Qatar.
48. *Al-Watan*, July 22, 1985, p. 1.
49. *Al-Qabas*, July 10, 1985, p. 4.
50. *Al-Qabas*, July 16, 1985, p. 4.
51. *Al-Qabas*, July 11, 1985, p. 4.
52. *Al-Qabas*, July 10, 1985, p. 1.
53. *Al-Qabas*, July 9, 1985, p. 1.
54. *Al-Qabas*, June 13, 1985, p. 2. Emphasis in original.
55. *Al-Qabas*, May 22, 1985, p. 2.
56. *Al-Qabas*, July 6, 1985, p. 2.
57. Ibid.

6
THE GCC AND THE FUTURE: CHALLENGES AND PROSPECTS

Research for this study has revealed that different segments of Gulf societies have differing perceptions of the Gulf Cooperation Council as a regional organization. These perceptions in fact reflect the enormous challenges facing the GCC in its attempts to coordinate the economic, political, and security activities of six traditional, Arab, Muslim states. These perceptions surface in statements that are frequently made by representatives of these societal segments. Consider the following as illustrative of these attitudes.

In his opening remarks before the sixteenth ordinary session of the GCC Ministerial Council (Saudi Arabia, September 2-3, 1985), the Kuwaiti foreign minister, Shaikh Sabah al-Ahmad al-Jabir, stated that in only four years, the GCC has made its presence felt on the international scene. This presence was evidenced by the activities of the GCC on the regional level (attempts to mediate the Iraq-Iran war), the Arab level (efforts to effect rapprochement between Iraq and Syria and between Syria and Jordan), and the international level (trade negotiations with the European Economic Community).[1] The communiqué issued following the Ministerial Council's meeting also underscored the presence of the GCC as an organization for regional understanding and peace.[2]

Statements with a different vein have also been made. For example, following a recent meeting of the directors of public relations in GCC ministries of the interior, a newspaper commentator urged the assembled directors to address the real issue before the GCC, namely the fear which the people have of the security forces. He defined the problem as being a crisis of confidence between rulers and subjects. The writer implied that the GCC cannot succeed in its long-term goal of enhancing the region's security unless GCC citizens can accept the legitimacy of the security forces in individual GCC countries. "We need institutions which preserve the integrity of the people before they serve the interests of government authorities."[3]

The other genre of statements about the GCC that emerged in the research reflect cynicism toward the organization. Illustrative examples include the following: When an average person is asked about his attitude toward the GCC, he sarcastically replies: "What GCC?" Second, when told that a study is being prepared about the GCC, a high government official in a GCC country replies cynically: "What can be written about the GCC?" Third, when asked for an opinion on the GCC, a successful Gulf merchant responds with one eloquent colloquial word: "*Hatchi!*," meaning "just talk." A fourth example involves a comment by a Gulf intellectual: "The GCC is a coordinated media blitz to preserve the present regimes in power."

What these statements indicate are the magnitude and multiplicity of challenges that the GCC faces and that it must overcome if it is to endure as a regional organization. However, before discussing these challenges, several comments are in order.

First, some of these challenges fall within the purview of the states themselves; they become GCC challenges only insofar as the organization is an extension of the states. This means that the member states must initiate certain domestic policies in the political and economic fields to address some of these internal challenges. Second, some of these challenges are outside the influence of the GCC as an organization. Third, while some of these challenges might be awesome, the GCC is a young organization founded in the midst of regional crises that have yet to dissipate. Fourth, some of the challenges that emanate from the realities of the member states, such as the small size of the countries and their small populations, cannot be meaningfully addressed in the foreseeable future.

With these comments as background, four areas of challenge may be identified: structure, leadership, objectives, and political ideology.

FIRST CHALLENGE: STRUCTURE

The Kuwaiti public opinion poll about the GCC, cited in Chapter 5, revealed that Gulf citizens would like to see the GCC expand to include the three other Gulf Arab states: Iraq and the two Yemens.

Since that was not the original intention of the GCC's founding fathers, present GCC leaders will have to face this popular demand. For the present, it might be easy to argue against extending GCC membership to Iraq and to South Yemen (PDRY). Iraq could be excluded on the grounds of its continued war with Iran, and PDRY could be excluded because of the state's Marxist ideology, viewed as repugnant to member states' traditional Islam. It is more difficult to argue against the membership of North Yemen. However, the GCC Charter itself does not provide for expandable membership. The Charter clearly states that the GCC is comprised of only those states whose leaders met at Abu Dhabi in May 1981. They were six states—tribal, traditional, and family-ruled.

Perhaps the intent of the founders was to exclude states other than the Kingdom and the emirates. If so, this intent should be clearly explained in the face of continued demands to widen the membership. The success of the GCC might well be a function of the basic social, economic, and cultural similarities of the membership. Diversity in these areas might therefore lead to divisiveness. In fact, the homogeneity of the present six states—cultural, historical, economic, and political—has been an essential ingredient of the GCC. This homogeneity does not extend to the other Arab states of the Gulf.

Another aspect of the structural challenge applies to the GCC organizational chart. As was pointed out above, Article 4 of the GCC Charter identifies the economic well-being of the peoples of the Gulf as the primary objective of the organization, yet the Ministerial Council of the GCC consists of the foreign ministers of the member states. No standing GCC council or structure has been established for the GCC ministers of planning, industry, or finance. To the average person, economic coordination, cooperation, and integration do not fall within the purview of the foreign ministers. When questioned on this point, one GCC citizen said that between early 1981 and late 1985, the Ministerial Council held at least 17 regular sessions without much progress toward economic integration. If the GCC wishes to be true to the objectives stated in its Charter, particularly Article 4, then perhaps a different ministerial council should be constituted.

SECOND CHALLENGE: LEADERSHIP

According to the organizational chart, the GCC is a pyramidal structure with authority flowing vertically, top to bottom. The GCC heads of state (Supreme Council) occupy the apex of this pyramid.

Below them is the Ministerial Council, consisting of the six foreign ministers. Administratively, the GCC is managed by the Secretariat, headed by the secretary general. This bureaucracy, which is headquartered in Riyadh, Saudi Arabia, has expanded considerably since the creation of the GCC; it has almost developed a life of its own.

The Supreme Council is not accountable for its actions to anyone. In this regard, the GCC is an extension of the centralized political structures that exist in the member states. In these states power is concentrated in the hands of the ruler with no organized popular input. With its popularly elected National Assembly, Kuwait is an exception. The Kuwaiti case is a double-edged sword: It forces the Kuwaiti leaders to be accountable to the National Assembly, and it challenges the other leaders to open up the GCC for popular input. This dilemma of rulers versus people is not likely to disappear; on the contrary, the successful democratic experiment in Kuwait is likely to exarcerbate this dilemma.

In addressing this challenge, GCC leaders might consider one of several options: (a) Do nothing and argue that differences in the political systems within the member states are tolerable and should not be detrimental to regional cooperation; (b) initiate steps to bring about more participation in the making of policy through the route of consultative assemblies which would be appointed by the ruler; (c) initiate plans for some sort of popularly elected national assemblies, which seems highly unlikely at this juncture of Gulf history except perhaps for Bahrain; or (d) exert more collective pressure on the Kuwaiti ruling family to limit the role of the Kuwaiti National Assembly as a partner in the making of public policy. To some Gulf intellectuals, this last option is frighteningly possible, particularly if regional terrorism continues unabated. The ongoing Iraq-Iran war, the proximity of Kuwait to Iran, and the possibility of an Iranian attack against Kuwait might provide the Kuwaiti ruling family with the proper incentive either to dissolve the National Assembly, as was done in 1976, or to curtail its powers severely.

THIRD CHALLENGE: OBJECTIVES

A definite gap exists in the minds of many Gulf citizens between the official rhetoric of GCC officials and the real accomplishments of the GCC. Article 4 of the Charter defines the basic objectives as involving coordination, cooperation, and integration in many fields including economics, finance, commerce, education, communications, and education. To underscore these objectives, the Unified Economic Agreement was approved only a few months after the adoption of the Charter. Nothing in the original Charter dealt with security.

However, the bulk of GCC activities and official statements have focused on security issues. As was mentioned in Chapter 2 above, security issues have ranged from exchange of sensitive data to joint military exercises. Again, a credibility gap has emerged regarding security as well.

In the economic sphere, several factors have contributed to the prevalent cynicism:

First, the implementation of most provisions of the Unified Economic Agreement has been extremely slow and in some areas nonexistent. Businessmen in different GCC countries have yet to feel the impact of the Unified Economic Agreement, particularly in regard to the exemption of national products from tariffs.

Second, regional economic planning remains an illusive goal. Member states are urged to coordinate their economic planning with each other, but not much has been done either in industrial planning or in development.

Third, no coordination has occurred regarding expatriate labor, either. Yet all economic studies, long-term and short-term, have pointed to expatriate labor as the major issue facing the Gulf states over the next two decades. A recent study on this question made it amply clear that the problem of expatriate labor can be solved only through a concerted regional effort.[4]

Fourth, nor have the GCC states developed any serious plans in preparation for the post-oil era. Such lack of coordination also applies to the present stage, particularly the investment of oil revenues.

Cynicism regarding the GCC's accomplishments in the security sphere has also been fueled by several factors. In spite of numerous official statements about the desire of the GCC states to become solely responsible for the security of the Gulf through self-reliance, the GCC has been unable to influence the course of the Iraq-Iran war or to minimize the potential Iranian threat inside the Gulf. The GCC must continue to rely on outside powers, such as the United States, to protect the Gulf should it face a serious regional threat.

Nor has the GCC agreed on standardization of their weapon systems or arms purchases. To the average GCC citizen, all the official rhetoric notwithstanding, the GCC states would find it almost impossible to repel an outside attack should one come either from Iran in the east or from Israel in the north. The large amounts of sophisticated weapons that the GCC countries have purchased in recent years have not improved their security appreciably.

FOURTH CHALLENGE: POLITICAL IDEOLOGY

Many Gulf citizens perceive the GCC, rightly or wrongly, as an organization of leaders for the preservation of the present regimes. It is an organization committed to protecting the status quo and to preventing change from invading the body politic of these societies. As an organization of leaders and not of peoples, the GCC is viewed as a vehicle for the perpetuation of family rule, both as a philosophy of government and a political ideology. In this context, there is no room for genuine change or for individual initiative or input. The studies examined in Chapter 4 above have raised serious questions, which cannot be ignored by GCC policymakers.

Two opposing ideologies seem to be emerging: One favors the status quo, the other advocates change. The first ideology is essentially authoritarian and maintains that security can be maintained through strong regimes. The other ideology argues that genuine security can be achieved through a democratization of family rule, as is the case in Kuwait. If this challenge is not addressed satisfactorily by the GCC, a clash between the two ideologies will become likely, thus destabilizing the very area the GCC is interested in protecting.

The Gulf Cooperation Council is a relatively young organization, the first of its kind in the Arab world. It has promise, but it faces major challenges. Once the GCC is transformed into an organization in which the Gulf citizen can nurture his aspirations for a life of dignity and economic prosperity, then it will become a major regional organization, and it will endure for many years.

NOTES

1. *Al-Qabas*, September 3, 1985, p. 2.
2. *Al-Qabas*, September 4, 1985, p. 2.
3. *Al-Watan*, September 18, 1985, p. 15.
4. *Al-Watan*, September 14, 1985, p. 7.

Appendix A

The States of

United Arab Emirates

State of Bahrain

Kingdom of Saudi Arabia

Sultanate of Oman

State of Qatar

State of Kuwait

Being fully aware of their mutual bonds and special relations, common characteristics and similar systems founded on the Creed of Islam; and

Based on their faith in the common destiny and destination that link their peoples; and

In view of their desire to effect coordination, integration and cooperation among them in all fields; and

Based on their conviction that coordination, cooperation and integration among them serve the higher goals of the Arab nation; and

In order to strengthen their cooperation and reinforce their common links; and

In an endeavor to complement efforts already begun in all vital fields that concern their peoples and realize their hopes in a better future on the path to unity of their states; and

In conformity with the Charter of the League of Arab States which calls for the realization of closer relations and stronger bonds; and

In order to channel their efforts to reinforce and serve Arab and Islamic causes

Have agreed as follows:

ARTICLE ONE

Establishment of Council

A council shall be established hereby to be named "The Cooperation Council for the Arab States of the Gulf," hereinafter referred to as the "Cooperation Council."

ARTICLE TWO

Headquarters

The Cooperation Council shall have its headquarters in Riyadh, Saudi Arabia.

ARTICLE THREE

Cooperation Council Meetings

The Council shall hold its meetings in the state where it has its headquarters, and may convene in any member state.

ARTICLE FOUR

Objectives

The basic objectives of the Cooperation Council are:

1. To effect coordination, integration and cooperation between member states in all fields in order to achieve unity among them.
2. To deepen and strengthen relations, links and scopes of cooperation now prevailing between their peoples in various fields.
3. To formulate similar regulations in verious fields including the following:
   a. Economics and finance
   b. Commerce, customs and communications
   c. Education and culture
   d. Social and health affairs
   e. Information and tourism
   f. Legislation and administrative affairs.
4. To stimulate scientific and technological progress in the fields of industry, minerology, agriculture, water and animal resources; to establish scientific research centers; to implement common projects, and to encourage cooperation by the private sector for for good of their peoples.

ARTICLE FIVE

Council Membership

The Cooperation Council shall be formed of the six states that participated in the Foreign Ministers' meeting held at Riyadh on February 4, 1981.

ARTICLE SIX

Structures of the Cooperation Council

The Cooperation Council shall have the following main structures:

1. Supreme Council to which shall be attached the Commission for Settlement of Disputes.
2. Ministerial Council.
3. Secretariat-General.

Each of these structures may establish branch organs as necessary.

ARTICLE SEVEN

Supreme Council

1. The Supreme Council is the highest authority of the Cooperation Council and shall be formed of heads of member states. Its presidency shall rotate alphabetically according to the names of the member states.
2. The Supreme Council shall hold one regular session every year. Extraordinary sessions may be convened at the request of any member seconded by another member.
3. The Supreme Council shall hold its sessions in the territory of member states.
4. A Supreme Council meeting shall be considered valid if attended by two thirds of the member states.

ARTICLE EIGHT

Supreme Council's Functions

The Supreme Council shall endeavor to achieve the objectives of the Cooperation Council, particularly concerning the following:

1. Review matters of interest to the member states.
2. Lay down the higher policy for the Cooperation Council and the basic lines it should follow.
3. Review the recommendations, reports, studies and common projects submitted by the Ministerial Council for approval.
4. Review reports and studies which the Secretary-General is charged to prepare.
5. Approve the bases for dealing with other states and international organizations.
6. Approve the rules of procedure of the Commission for Settlement of Disputes and nominate its members.
7. Appoint the Secretary-General.
8. Amend the Charter of the Cooperation Council.
9. Approve the Council's Internal Rules.
10. Approve the budget of the Secretariat-General.

ARTICLE NINE

Voting in Supreme Council

1. Each member of the Supreme Council shall have one vote.
2. Resolutions of the Supreme Council on substantive matters shall be carried by unanimous approval of the member states participating in the voting, while resolutions on procedural matters shall be carried by a majority vote.

ARTICLE TEN

Commission for Settlement of Disputes

1. The Cooperation Council shall have a commission called "Commission for Settlement of Disputes," which shall be attached to the Supreme Council.
2. The Supreme Council shall form the Commission for every case separately based on the nature of the dispute.
3. If a dispute arises over interpretation or implementation of the Charter and such dispute is not resolved within the ministerial Council or the Supreme Council, the Supreme Council may refer such dispute to the Commission for Settlement of Disputes.
4. The Commission shall submit its recommendations or opinion, as applicable, to the Supreme Council for appropriate action.

ARTICLE ELEVEN

Ministerial Council

1. The Ministerial Council shall consist of the Foreign Ministers of the member states or other delegated Ministers. The Council's presidency shall rotate among members every three months by alphabetical order of the states.
2. The Ministerial Council shall convene every three months and may hold extraordinary sessions at the invitation of any member seconded by another member.
3. The Ministerial Council shall decide the venue of its next session.
4. A Council's meeting shall be deemed valid if attended by two thirds of the member states.

ARTICLE TWELVE

Functions of the Ministerial Council

The Ministerial Council's functions shall include the following:

1. Propose policies, prepare recommendations, studies and projects aimed at developing cooperation and coordination among member states in the various fields and adopt required resolutions or appropriate recommendations.
2. Endeavor to encourage, develop and coordinate activities between member states in all fields. Resolutions adopted in such matters shall be referred to the Ministerial Council for further submission, with recommendations, to the Supreme Council for appropriate action.
3. Submit recommendations to the Ministers concerned to formulate policies whereby the Cooperation Council's resolutions may be put into action.
4. Encourage means of cooperation and coordination between the various private sector activities, develop cooperation between the member states' chambers of commerce and industry, and encourage flow of working citizens of the member states among them.

5. Refer any of the various facets of cooperation to one or more technical or specialized committees for study and presentation of relevant proposals.
6. Review proposals related to amendments to this Charter and submit appropriate recommendations to the Supreme Council.
7. Approve the Ministerial Council's Rules of Procedure as well as the Rules of Procedure of the Secretariat-General.
8. Appoint the Assistant Secretaries-General, as nominated by the Secretary-General, for a renewable period of three years.
9. Approve periodic reports as well as internal rules and regulations related to administrative and financial affairs proposed by the Secretary General, and submit recommendations to the Supreme Council for approval of the budget of the Secretariat General.
10. Make arrangements for the Supreme Council's meetings and prepare their agendas.
11. Review matters referred to it by the Supreme Council.

ARTICLE THIRTEEN

Voting in Ministerial Council

1. Every member of the Ministerial Council shall have one vote.
2. Resolutions of the Ministerial Council on substantive matters shall be carried by a unanimous vote of the member states present and voting, and on the procedural matters by a majority vote.

ARTICLE FOURTEEN

Secretariat-General

1. The Secretariat-General shall be composed of a Secretary-General who shall be assisted by deputies and a number of staff as required.
2. The Supreme Council shall appoint the Secretary-General, who shall be a citizen of one of the Cooperation Council states, for a period of three years which may be renewed for one time only.
3. The Secretary-General shall nominate the assistant secretaries-general.
4. The Secretary-General shall appoint the Secretariat-General's staff from among the citizens of member states and may not make exceptions with the approval of the Ministerial Council.
5. The Secretary-General shall be directly responsible for the work of the Secretariat-General and the smooth flow of work in its various organizations. He shall represent the Cooperation Council with other parties within the powers vested in him.

ARTICLE FIFTEEN

Functions of the Secretariat-General

The Secretariat-General shall undertake the following functions:

1. Prepare studies related to cooperation and coordination, integration and programs for member states' common action.
2. Prepare periodic reports on the Cooperation Council's work.
3. Follow up the implementation by the member states of the resolutions and recommendations of the Supreme Council and Ministerial Council.
4. Prepare reports and studies ordered by the Supreme Council or Ministerial Council.
5. Prepare the draft of administrative and financial regulations commensurate with the growth of the Cooperation Council and its expanding responsibilities.
6. Prepare the Cooperation Council's budgets and accounts.
7. Make preparations for meetings, prepare agendas and draft resolutions for the Ministerial Council.
8. Recommend to the Chairman of the Ministerial Council the convening of extraordinary sessions of the Council whenever necessary.
9. Perform any other tasks entrusted to it by the Supreme Council or Ministerial Council.

ARTICLE SIXTEEN

The Secretary-General, the assistant secretaries-general and all members of the Secretariat-General's staff shall carry out their duties in complete independence and for the common interest of the member states.

They shall refrain from any action or behavior that is incompatible with their duties and from divulging the secrets of their jobs either during or after their tenure of office.

ARTICLE SEVENTEEN

Privileges and Immunities

1. The Cooperation Council and its organizations shall enjoy on the territories of all member states such legal competence, privileges and immunities as required to realize their objectives and carry out their functions.
2. Representatives of the member states on the Council and the Council's employees, shall enjoy such privileges and immunities as are specified in agreements to be concluded for this purpose among the member states.
   A special agreement shall organize the relations between the Council and the state in which it has its headquarters.
3. Until such time as the two agreements mentioned in item 2 above are prepared and put into effect, the representatives of the member states in the Cooperation Council and its staff shall enjoy the diplomatic privileges and immunities established for similar organizations.

ARTICLE EIGHTEEN

Budget of the Secretariat-General

The Secretariat-General shall have a budget to which the member states shall contribute equal amounts.

ARTICLE NINETEEN

Charter Implementation

1. This Charter shall go into effect as of the date it is signed by the heads of the six member states named in this Charter's Preamble.
2. The original copy of this Charter shall be deposited with Saudi Arabia's Ministry of Foreign Affairs which shall deliver a true copy thereof to every member state, pending the establishment of the Secretariat-General at which time the latter shall become depository.

ARTICLE TWENTY

Amendments to Charter

1. Any member state may request an amendment to this Charter.
2. Requests for Charter amendments shall be submitted to the Secretary-General who shall refer them to the member states at least four months prior to submission to the Ministerial Council.
3. An amendment shall become effective if it is approved unanimously by the Supreme Council.

ARTICLE TWENTY-ONE

Closing Provisions

No reservations may be voiced with respect to the provisions of this Charter.

ARTICLE TWENTY-TWO

The Secretariat-General shall arrange to deposit and register copies of this Charter with the League of Arab States and the United Nations, by resolution of the Ministerial Council.

This Charter is signed on one copy in Arabic at Abu Dhabi City, United Arab Emirates, on 21 Rajab 1401 corresponding to May 25, 1981.

United Arab Emirates

State of Bahrain

Kingdom of Saudi Arabia

Sultanate of Oman

State of Qatar

State of Kuwait

Appendix B

With the help of God the Almighty;

The Governments of the member states of the Gulf Cooperation Council;

In accordance with the Charter thereof, which calls for closer cooperation and stronger links; and,

Desiring to promote, expand and enhance their economic ties on solid foundations, in the best interest of their peoples; and,

Intending to coordinate and unify their economic, financial and monetary policies, as well as their commercial and industrial legislation and customs regulations, have agreed as follows:

CHAPTER ONE

TRADE EXCHANGE

Article 1

a. The member states shall permit the importation and exportation among each other of agricultural, animal, industrial and natural resource products that are of national origin.
b. All agricultural, animal, industrial and natural resource products that are of national origin shall receive the same treatment as national products.

Article 2

1. All agricultural, animal, industrial and natural resource products that are of national origin shall be exempted from customs duties and other charges having equivalent effect.
2. Fees charged for specific services such as demurrage, storage, transportation, haulage or unloading, shall not be considered as customs duties when they are levied on domestic products.

Article 3

1. For products of national origin to qualify as national products, the value added ensuing from their production in members states shall not be less than 40% of their final value. In addition, the share of the member states' citizens in the ownership of the producing plant shall not be less than 51%.
2. Every item to be exempted hereby shall be accompanied by a certificate of origin duly authenticated by the government agency concerned.

Article 4

1. Member states shall establish a uniform minimum customs tariff applicable to the products of third countries.
2. One of the objectives of the uniform customs tariff shall be the protection of national products from foreign competition.
3. The uniform customs tariff shall be applied gradually within five years from the date of entry into force of this agreement. Arrangements for the gradual application shall be agreed upon within one year from the said date.

Article 5

Member states shall grant all facilities for the transit of any member state's goods to other member states, exempting them from any duties and taxes, whatsoever, without prejudice to the provisions of Paragraph 2 of Article 2.

Article 6

Transit shall be denied to any goods that are barred from entry into the territory of a member state by its local regulations. Lists of such goods shall be exchanged between the customs authorities of the member states.

Article 7

Member states shall coordinate their commercial policies and relations with other states and regional economic groupings and blocs with a view toward creating balanced trade relations and favorable circumstances and terms of trade.

To achieve this goal, the member states shall make the following arrangements;

1. Coordinate export/import policies and regulations.
2. Coordinate policies for building up strategic food stocks.
3. Conclude economic agreements collectively when and if the common benefit of the member states is realized.
4. Work for the creation of a collective negotiating force to strengthen their negotiating position via-à-vis foreign parties in the field of importation of basic needs and exportation of major products.

CHAPTER TWO

MOVEMENT OF CAPITAL, CITIZENS AND EXERCISE OF ECONOMIC ACTIVITIES

Article 8

The member states shall agree on the executive rules which would ensure that each member state shall grant the citizens of all other member states the same treatment granted to its own citizens without any discrimination or differentiation in the following fields:

1. Freedom of movement, work and residence.
2. Right of ownership, inheritance and bequest.
3. Freedom of exercising economic activity.
4. Free movement of capital.

Article 9

The member states shall encourage their respective private sectors to establish joint ventures in order to link their citizens' economic interest in the various spheres.

CHAPTER THREE

COORDINATION OF DEVELOPMENT

Article 10

The member states shall endeavor to achieve coordination and harmony among their respective development plans with a view to achieving economic integration between them.

Article 11

1. The member states shall endeavor to coordinate their policies with regard to all aspects of the oil industry including extraction, refining, marketing, processing, pricing, exploitation of natural gas, and development of energy sources.
2. The member states shall endeavor to formulate unified oil policies and adopt common positions via-à-vis outside world, and in the international specialized organizations.

Article 12

To achieve the objectives specified in this Agreement, the member states shall perform the following:

1. Coordinate industrial activities, formulate policies and mechanisms aiming at the industrial development and the diversification of their productive bases and on integrated basis.
2. Standardize their industrial legislation and regulations and guide their local production units to meet their needs.
3. Allocate industries among member states according to relative advantages and economic feasibility, and encourage the establishment of basic as well as ancillary industries.

Article 13

Within the framework of coordination, the member states shall pay special attention to the establishment of joint ventures in the fields of industry, agriculture and services, and shall support them with public, private or mixed capital in order to achieve economic integration, productive interfaces, and common development on a sound economic basis.

CHAPTER FOUR

TECHNICAL COOPERATION

Article 14

The member states shall collaborate in finding spheres for common technical cooperation aimed at building a genuine local base founded on encouragement and support of research and applied sciences and technology as well as adapting imported technology to meet the region's progress and development objectives.

Article 15

Member states shall set rules, make arrangements and lay down terms for the transfer of technology, selecting the most suitable or introducing such changes thereto as would serve their various needs. Member states shall also, whenever feasible, conclude uniform agreements with foreign governments and scientific or commercial firms to achieve these objectives.

Article 16

The member states shall formulate policies and implement coordinated programs for technical, vocational and professional training and rehabilitation at all levels and stages. They shall also upgrade educational curricula at all levels to link education and technology with the development needs of the member states.

Article 17

The member states shall coordinate their manpower policies and shall formulate uniform and standardized criteria and classification for the various categories of occupations and crafts in different sectors in order to avoid harmful competition among themselves and to optimize the utilization of available human resources.

CHAPTER FIVE

TRANSPORT AND COMMUNICATION

Article 18

The member states shall accord means for passenger and cargo transportation belonging to citizens of the other member states, when transiting or entering their territory, the same treatment they accord to the means of passenger and cargo transportation belong to their own citizens, including exemption from all duties and taxes, whatsoever. However, local transportations are excluded.

Article 19

1. The member states shall cooperate in the fields of land and sea transportation, and communications. They shall also coordinate and establish infrastructure projects such as seaports, airports, water and power stations, roads, with a view to realizing common economic development and linking their economic activities with each other.
2. The member states shall coordinate aviation and air transport policies among them and promote all spheres of joint activities at various levels.

Article 20

The member states shall allow steamers, ships and boats and their cargoes, belonging to any member state to freely use the various port facilities and grant them the same treatment and privileges granted to their own in docking or calling at the ports as concerns fees, pilotage, and docking services, haulage, loading and unloading, maintenance, repair, storage of goods and other similar services.

CHAPTER SIX

FINANCIAL AND MONETARY COOPERATION

Article 21

The member states shall seek to unify investment in order to achieve a common investment policy aimed at directing their internal and external investments towards serving their interest, and realizing their peoples' aspirations in development and progress.

Article 22

The member states shall seek to coordinate their financial, monetary agencies and central banks, including an endeavor to establish a common currency in order to further their desired economic integration.

Article 23

Member states shall seek to coordinate their external policies in the sphere of international and regional development aid.

CHAPTER SEVEN

CLOSING PROVISIONS

Article 24

In the execution of the Agreement and determination of the procedures resulting therefrom, consideration shall be given to differences in the levels of development between the member states and the local development priorities of each. Any member state may be temporarily exempted from applying such provisions of this Agreement as may be necessitated by temporary local situations in that state or specific circumstances faced by it. Such exemption shall be for a specified period and shall be decided by the Supreme Council of the Gulf Cooperation Council.

Article 25

No member state shall give to any non-member state any preferential privilege exceeding that given herein.

Article 26

a. This Agreement shall enter into force four months after its approval by the Supreme Council.
b. This Agreement may be amended by consent from the Supreme Council.

Article 27

In case of conflict with local laws and regulations of member states, execution of the provisions of this Agreement shall prevail.

Article 28

Provisions herein shall supersede any similar provisions contained in bilateral agreements.

Drawn up at Riyadh on 6 Sha'ban 1401 Corresponding to June 8, 1981.

Appendix C

Name	*Position*	*Country*
Usama Abd al-Rahman	Dean, College of Public Administration, University of Riyadh	Saudi Arabia
Ahmad Ali Du'ayj	Chairman of the Board, Kuwait Real Estate and Investment Group	Kuwait
Turki bin Khalid al-Sudayri	Director of Civil Service	Saudi Arabia
Jamil Abdallah al-Jishi	Director, Jubayl Project	Saudi Arabia
Hasan Abdallah Fakhro	Director, Bahrain National Oil Company	Bahrain
Said Ahmad Ghabbash	Minister of Planning, Abu Dhabi	United Arab Emirates
Sulayman Abd al-Razzaq al-Mutawwa'	Vice President, Foundation for the South and the Arabian Gulf	Kuwait
Sayf Ahmad al-Gharir	Chairman, Chambers of Commerce, Industry and Agriculture	United Arab Emirates
Abdallah Jum'a al-Kabisi	Lecturer, University of Qatar	Qatar
Abdallah Muhammad al-Nibari	Secretary, Kuwait Economic Society	Kuwait
Abd al-Baqi Abdallah al-Nuri	Chairman of the Board, Petrochemical Industries Company	Kuwait
Abdallah Yusif al-Ghanim	Former Minister of Electricity	Kuwait
Abd al-Rahman bin Muhammad al-Sadhan	Secretary-General, Civil Service Council	Saudi Arabia
Abd al-Rahman Abdallah al-Zamil	Chief Executive Officer, Electricity Company of the South Western Province	Saudi Arabia
Abd al-Aziz Rashid al-Rashid	President, Rashid Group (Accountants and Legal Consultants)	Saudi Arabia
Abd al-Aziz al-Sultan	Deputy Director, Kuwait Engineering Office	Kuwait

Name	*Position*	*Country*
Abd al-Aziz Abdallah al-Zamil	Deputy Director, Saudi Basic Industries Company	Saudi Arabia
Abd al-Wahhab Ali al-Tammar	Chief Executive Officer, Kuwait Investment and Foreign Trade Company	Kuwait
Ali Khalifa al-Kuwari	Director, Development Study Project	Qatar
Ali Badr al-Rahman al-Khalaf	Secretary-General, Gulf Organization for Industrial Investments	Qatar
Ghanim Faris al-Mazru'i	Secretary-General, Abu Dhabi Investment Project	United Arab Emirates
Faruq Abdallah Ni'meh	Director of Public Relations and Personnel, Qatari Foundation for Oil Production	Qatar
Fahd bin Saud al-Dughaythir	Chief Executive Officer, Saudi Real Estate Company	Saudi Arabia
Mahmud Hamra Kruha	Director, Abu Dhabi National Oil Company	United Arab Emirates
Mu'ayyad Abd al-Aziz al-Rashid	Deputy Assistant for Industrial Affairs, Ministry of Industry and Commerce	Kuwait
Yusif Ibrahim al-Ghanim	Chief Executive Officer, Heavy Equipment Company	Kuwait

Bibliography

Abdulgani, J. M. *Iraq and Iran: The Years of Crisis*. Baltimore, MD: The Johns Hopkins University Press, 1984.

Annual Report 1404 (1984). Riyadh, Saudi Arabia: Saudi Arabian Monetary Agency, 1984.

The Atlantic Council. *Oil and Turmoil: Western Policies in the Middle East*. Washington, DC, September 1979.

_______. *After Afghanistan–The Long Haul*. Washington, DC, March 1980.

Al-Baharna, Husain M. *The Legal Status of the Arabian Gulf States*. 2nd edition. Beirut, Lebanon: Librairie du Liban, 1975.

Beblawi, Hazem. *The Arab Gulf Economy in a Turbulent Age*. London: Croom Helm, 1984.

Bishara, Abdallah. "We Don't Need Volunteers to Protect Our House." *The Middle East* (London), November 1983, pp. 13-17.

Chubin, Shahram. *Soviet Policy Toward Iran and the Gulf*. Adelphi Papers, no. 157. London: International Institute for Strategic Studies, 1980.

Cordesman, Anthony H. *The Gulf and the Search for Strategic Stability*. Boulder, CO: Westview Press, 1984.

Cottrell, Alvin. *The Persian Gulf States*. Baltimore, Maryland: The Johns Hopkins University Press, 1980.

Darius, Robert G. et al., eds. *Gulf Security into the 1980s: Perceptual and Strategic Dimensions*. Stanford, CA: Hoover Institution Press, 1984.

Dawisha, Adeed. *Saudi Arabia's Search for Security*. Adelphi Papers, No. 158. London: International Institute for Strategic Studies, 1979.

Dessouki, Ali E. H. *The Iraq-Iran War: Issues of Conflict and Prospects for Settlement*. Princeton, NJ: Princeton University, Center for International Studies, 1981.

Duignan, Peter, and L. H. Gann. *The Middle East and North Africa: The Challenge to Western Security*. Stanford, CA: Hoover Institution Press, 1981.

El-Azhary, M. S. *The Gulf Cooperation Council and Regional Defense in the 1980s*. Exeter, England: University of Exeter Press, 1982.

Esposito, John L., ed. *Voices of Resurgent Islam*. New York: Oxford University Press, 1983.

Heller, Mark, ed. *The Middle East Military Balance, 1984*. Tel Aviv, Israel: Tel Aviv University, 1984.

Heller, Mark and N. Safran. *The New Middle Class and Regime Stability in Saudi Arabia*. Cambridge, MA: Harvard University, Middle East Papers, 1985.

Hunter, Shireen, ed. *Gulf Cooperation Council: Problems and Prospects*. Washington, DC: Center for Strategic and International Studies, 1984.

Ibrahim, Ibrahim. *Arab Resources: The Transformation of a Society*. Washington, DC: Center for Contemporary Arab Studies, 1983.

Jaidah, Ali M. *An Appraisal of OPEC Oil Policies*. London: Longman, 1983.

Khalifa, Ali Mohammed. *The United Arab Emirates: Unity in Fragmentation*. Boulder, CO: Westview Press, 1979.

Martin, Lenore G. *The Unstable Gulf*. Lexington, MA: Lexington Books, 1984.

The Middle East Institute. *The Gulf and the Peninsula: American Interests and Policies in the Eighties*. Washington, DC: 34th Annual Conference, September 1980.

The Middle East and North Africa, 1984-85. London: Europa Publications, 1984.

Middle East Oil and Gas. New York: Exxon Corporation, 1984.

The Military Balance, 1984-1985. London: International Institute for Strategic Studies, 1984.

Nakhleh, Emile A. *The Persian Gulf and American Policy*. New York: Praeger, 1982.

Niblock, Tim and Richard Lawless, eds. *Prospects for the World Oil Industry*. London: Croom Helm, 1985.

Niblock, Tim, ed. *Social and Economic Development in the Arab Gulf*. London: Croom Helm, 1980.

Noyes, James H. *The Clouded Lens: Persian Gulf Security and U.S. Policy*. Stanford, CA: Hoover Institution Press, 1979.

Ottaway, David. "Persian Gulf War Posing New Threat to U.S. Interests." *Washington Post*. September 27, 1985.

Peterson, J. E. ed. *The Politics of Middle East Oil*. Washington, DC: Middle East Institute, 1983.

Quandt, William B. *Saudi Arabia in the 1980s: Foreign Policy, Security, and Oil*. Washington, DC: Brookings Institution, 1981.

Roucek, Joseph S. and M. V. Belok. *United States and the Persian Gulf*. Malabar, Florida: Robert E. Krieger Publishing Company, 1985.

Rubin, Barry. *Paved with Good Intentions: The American Experience and Iran*. London and New York: Oxford University Press, 1980.

Sayigh, Yusif A. *Arab Oil Policies in the 1970s*. Baltimore, Maryland: The Johns Hopkins University Press, 1983.

Shaw, John A. and D. E. Long. *Saudi Arabian Modernization Impact of Change on Stability*. Washington, DC: Center for Strategic and International Studies, 1982. The Washington Papers/189.

Sivard, Ruth Leger. *World Military and Social Expenditures 1983*. Washington, DC: World Priorities, 1983.

The Smoldering Fires Along the Gulf. Bonn, Germany: Friedrich Ebert Stiftung Research Institute, 1982.

Stempel, John D. *Inside the Iranian Revolution*. Bloomington: Indiana University Press, 1981.

Strategic Survey, 1984-1985. London: The International Institute for Strategic Studies, 1984.

World Military Expenditures and Arms Transfers, 1985. Washington, DC: U.S. Arms Control and Disarmament Agency, 1985.

Yorke, Valerie. *The Gulf in the 1980s*. London: Royal Institute of International Affairs, 1980.

ARABIC PUBLICATIONS

Abd al-Rahman, Usama. *Oil Bureaucracy and the Problem of Development*. Kuwait: National Council for Culture and the Arts, 1982.

Bisisu, Adnan. "Off-Shore Banking in Bahrain." Bahrain: Chamber of Commerce and Industry, 1984. Unpublished.

Cooperation Council for the Arab States of the Gulf. Riyadh, Saudi Arabia: Bahr al-Ulum Press, 1981.

Cooperation Council for the Arab States of the Gulf. Bahrain: Government Printing Office, 1983.

Documents of the Gulf Cooperation Council. Vol. IV. Doha, Qatar: Qatar News Agency, 1984.

Foreign Labor in the Gulf Arab States. Beirut, Lebanon: Center for the Study of Arab Unity, 1983.

"GCC Calls for Coordination Among Gulf News Agencies." *Saudi Press Agency*. Washington, DC: May 21, 1984.

Gulf Cooperation Council: Initial Steps Taken by the Member States for the Implementation of the Unified Economic Agreement. Riyadh, Saudi Arabia: GCC Secretariat, 1984.

Al-Isa, Shamlan Yusif and K. al-Manufi. *Trends in Kuwaiti Public Opinion Regarding the Gulf Cooperation Council*. University of Kuwait, Department of Political Science, 1985.

Al-Jalal, Abd al-Aziz. "The Arab Teacher: Training, Qualifications, and the Teaching Profession." Abu Dhabi, United Arab Emirates, 1984. Unpublished.

________. "Problems of the Educational System and Development." Abu Dhabi, United Arab Emirates, 1984. Unpublished.

________. "Role of Education in Development." Abu Dhabi, United Arab Emirates, 1984. Unpublished.

Al-Kuwari, Ali Khalifa. *Role of Publicly Owned Projects in Economic Development*. Beirut, Lebanon: Beirut Establishment for Printing and Binding, 1983.

Al-Musa, Ali. "Population Policy and the Future of Development in the Oil-Producing States of the Arabian Peninsula." Bahrain, 1985. Unpublished.

Al-Nafisi, Abdallah Fahd. *Gulf Cooperation Council: Political and Strategic Context*. London: Ta-Ha Publishers, 1982.

"Role of Industry in Building a Productive Base in the Oil-Producing States of the Arabian Peninsula." Kuwait: Industrial Consulting Office, 1983. Unpublished.

Al-Rumaihi, Muhammad. *Social and Economic Constraints of Development*. Kuwait: Kazima, 1977.

A Special Report Regarding the Convening of the Fifth Summit of the GCC States in Kuwait. Kuwait: Kuwait News Agency, November 1984.

The Unified Economic Agreement. Riyadh, Saudi Arabia: Gulf Cooperation Council Secretariat, 1981.

ARABIC ARTICLES

Al-Ash'al Abdallah. "International Relations in the Context of the GCC." *Journal of the Gulf and Arabian Peninsula Studies*, Vol. X, No. 37 (January 1984):61-89.

"Foreign Labor in the GCC Countries" *Industry and Petroleum News*, Vol. XVI, No. 177. (April 1985):18-20.

Ibrahim, Hasan. "The United States and the GCC: Cooperation or Confrontation?" *Al-Qabas*, November 21, 1984, p. 21.

Al-Khatib, Omar Ibrahim. "The Federal Experiment of the United Arab Emirates: Constitutional Provisions and Political Practice." *Journal of Social Sciences*, Vol. X, No. 4 (December 1982):185-233.

Al-Manufi, Kamal. "Political Culture and the Crisis of Democracy in the Arab World." *Al-Watan*, November 11, 1984.

Mutwalli, Mukhtar Muhammad and Abd al-Mahmud Abd al-Rahman. "Economic Development in the Gulf Cooperation Council States, 1970-1982." *Journal of the Gulf and Arabian Peninsula Studies*, Vol. XI, No. 43 (July 1985):113-40.

Index

About the Author

EMILE A. NAKHLEH is professor of political science and chairman of the Department of History and Political Science at Mount Saint Mary's College, Emmitsburg, Maryland. He is also an adjunct scholar at the American Enterprise Institute and the Georgetown University Center for Strategic and International Studies, Washington, DC. Professor Nakhleh was a Fulbright senior fellow (Bahrain, 1972-73), a National Endowment for the Humanities research fellow with residency at the American Enterprise Institute (Washington, DC, 1979-80), and a Woodrow Wilson guest scholar (Washington, DC, summer 1979). Dr. Nakhleh has traveled extensively in the Middle East, has lectured widely both in the United States and overseas, and has written and contributed to many books and journals. His recent books include *The Persian Gulf and American Policy* (1982); *A Palestinian Agenda for the West Bank and Gaza* (1980); *The West Bank and Gaza: Toward the Making of a Palestinian State* (1979); *Bahrain: Political Development in a Modernizing Society* (1976); *The United States and Saudi Arabia: A Policy Analysis* (1975); and *Arab-American Relations in the Persian Gulf* (1975).

www.ingramcontent.com/pod-product-compliance
Lightning Source LLC
LaVergne TN
LVHW011805200926
848484LV00003B/785
9780275921521